Opium

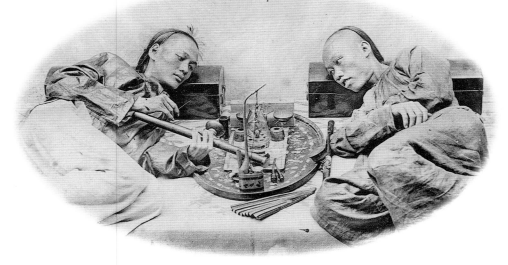

Fumerie d'opium.

Opium

A Portrait of the Heavenly Demon

Barbara Hodgson

GREYSTONE BOOKS
Douglas & McIntyre
Vancouver/Toronto/Berkeley

Greystone Books
A division of Douglas & McIntyre Ltd.
2323 Quebec Street, Suite 201
Vancouver, British Columbia
Canada V5T 4S7
www.greystonebooks.com

NATIONAL LIBRARY OF CANADA CATALOGUING IN PUBLICATION DATA
Hodgson, Barbara, 1955–
    Opium

    Includes bibliographical references and index.
    ISBN 1-55054-672-4 (bound)   1-55365-058-1 (pbk.)

    1. Opium habit—History.   2. Opium trade—History. I. Title.
HV5816.H62 1999   362.29´3   C98-910930-5

Library of Congress Cataloging-in-Publication data is available.

Editing by Saeko Usukawa
Design by Barbara Hodgson/Byzantium Books
Research assistance by Françoise Giovannangeli and David Gay
Printed and bound in China
Printed on acid-free paper
Distributed in the U.S. by Publishers Group West

We gratefully acknowledge the financial support of the Canada Council for the
Arts, the British Columbia Arts Council, and the Government of Canada
through the Book Publishing Industry Development Program (BPIDP) for our
publishing activities.

Half-title page: Fumerie d'opium (Opium Den). Postcard from the Territoire de Kouang-Tchéou-Wan, Indochina.

Frontispiece: Un vice nouveau (A New Vice). Opium smoking had been fashionable in French port cities since the 1890s, and by 1903 the habit had spread throughout France. *Le Petit Journal,* 5 July 1903.

Facing page: Opium poppy (Papaver somniferum). Copperplate engraving by A. Bell, the *Encyclopædia Britannica,* 1797.

Papaver Somniferum.

CONTENTS

In the film *The Dividend* (U.S. 1916), a young man, upset that his busy father ignores him, visits an opium den and becomes addicted to the drug. By the time the father decides to help him, the son is too far gone and dies in his arms.[1] This appropriately debauched scene is outfitted with real opium pipes and lamps and conforms to descriptions of dens of the day. Directed by Walter Edwards and with a screenplay by C. Gardner Sullivan, it starred Charles Ray, Ethel Ullman and William H. Thompson. *Courtesy BFI Stills, Posters and Designs*

"One must not think life with the mind, but with opium."—André Malraux, *Man's Fate*[1]

INTRODUCTION

"O just, subtle, and all-conquering opium!"
—Thomas De Quincey, *Confessions of an English Opium-Eater*[2]

Opium: potent and evocative, it is a word with the power to intoxicate both speaker and listener, a word that implies languor, mystery and a sort of sinister beauty. Nothing seems to capture the sensuousness of this word better than the image of the dreamy smoker adrift in his illicit paradise. Aside from the opium, he has few needs: a place to recline and the comforting proximity of fellow habitués. Lost in a cloud of visions, inseparable from his pipe, released from the cares and worries of everyday life, he has chosen opium to be his faithful friend, his lifelong companion. But this hedonistic picture has faded into the past. For although opium smoking still exists in isolated communities, the nineteenth-century fashion—or epidemic, as some have called it—that alarmed governments and citizens for almost a century has all but died away.

Possibly one of the most versatile drugs known thanks to its principal active ingredient, morphine, opium deadens

"Opium and Pipe smokers." The man seated on the left is posed holding a water pipe, the one on the right a tobacco pipe. The two men reclining are smoking opium. The boys flanking the opium smokers are probably attendants. Postcard from Hong Kong, c. 1890.

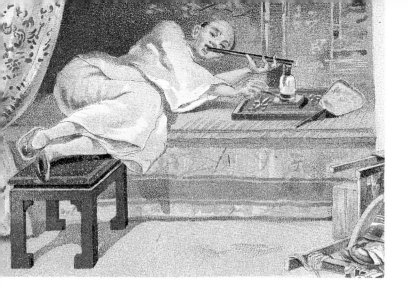

This page: Signore fumatore d'oppio (Opium Smoker). Lithograph from an Italian schoolbook, *I Popoli del Mondo: Usi e Costumi (People of the World, Traditions and Customs),* c. 1910.

Facing page: Ayer's Cherry Pectoral, trade card. Smoking was only one side of the opium addiction problem. A far wider spread phenomenon was found in the patent medicine trade. From the mid–nineteenth century until about 1910, thousands of American and British babies were raised on opium-laced soothing syrups designed to stop the crying brought on by weaning, teething or hunger. Opium was also used to treat cholera, dysentery, ague, bronchitis, earache, bedwetting, measles, morning sickness and piles. And cough syrups, such as Ayer's Cherry Pectoral, usually contained opium, since opium was and remains unsurpassed as a cough suppressant. Trade cards, distributed by the drug companies and pharmacists, were, and still are, popular collectibles.

pain, produces elation, induces sleep and reduces distress. In the long history of opium use around the world, people in search of euphoria and well-being have managed to introduce opium and its derivatives into the body in every way imaginable; in addition to being smoked, it has been drunk, eaten, sniffed, rubbed on and injected.

Whereas the opium smoker inhales the drug's vapours using a pipe specially designed for the purpose, the "opium-eater" drank it, usually in the form of laudanum, an opium-alcohol mixture; the true opium eater ingested it in the form of small pills often mixed with substances that disguised the bitter taste.

"A man who would use opium for every little trivial ache and pain would take an 80-ton gun to go rabbit shooting."—The Family Physician[3]

In the nineteenth century, opium was the prime ingredient in countless numbers of patent medicines that were used to quiet crying babies, calm frayed nerves and restore a semblance of health to millions.

Thomas De Quincey, author of the legendary *Confessions of an English Opium-Eater* (1821), remarked that unlike wine, which provides a "flickering flame" of pleasure, opium gives a "steady and equable glow." In those days opium was called a "stimulant," a term then used to describe something that produced a state of well-being, and not, as it is understood today, a state of excitement. Louis Lewin, in his 1931 book *Phantastica,* correctly identified opiates as drugs that sedated mental activity and classified them as "Euphorica." Today, opium is classified as a "narcotic," a drug that dulls the senses.[4]

Whatever means is used, to consume opium regularly, in any form, is to risk forging an almost unbreakable and deadly bond. Because opium is one of the most addictive and debilitating

CHINOIS FUMANT L'OPIUM. — Page 363.

"Opium-smoking is a sort of inclined plane, down which he who ventures to slide a little way is tolerably sure to go to the bottom."

—Anonymous, *Points and Pickings of Information about China and the Chinese*[5]

substances on earth, the opium addict—that is, the person dependent upon or habituated to opium—has been called slave, fiend and ghost.

Facing page: Chinois fumant l'opium (Chinese Smoking Opium). The original text reads: "The barbarians, servile and well trained, rarely depart from the humble airs reminiscent of slaves. Indolent, often reclining on flat sofas . . . they never let themselves show the slightest hint of passion, even when they are in the midst of the voluptuous effects of opium smoking." From *L'Univers illustré*, 13 October 1859, p. 364.

This page: An opium layout showing pipe, lamp, tins, spatula and needle. From *Three Years' Wanderings in the Northern Provinces of China* by Robert Fortune, 1847, p. 244.

Opium smoking was introduced to the West in the 1850s, a habit brought from China by European travellers and sailors, and Chinese immigrants. Veiled by an unrivalled aura of Eastern decadence, it appealed to those with an artistic temperament in Europe and to degenerates in North America. Adopted on the one hand by writers, artists and the wealthy who seemed to have little better to do with their time and money than squander it on bad habits, and, on the other, by sailors, prostitutes and drifters who seemed to have nothing but bad habits, opium smoking was relegated to society's fringes.

And, as if opium wasn't enough, cocaine, ether, hashish, chloroform and absinthe also became popular at around the same time. In fact, the consumption of all drugs in all forms

The French novelist Guy de Maupassant was an ether sniffer, and a number of French writers, including Théophile Gautier and Alexandre Dumas, experimented with hashish. The French poet Paul-Marie Verlaine and the English writer Oscar Wilde were habitual absinthe drinkers. In 1860, *The Illustrated London News* called absinthe the "opium of France" and remarked that it had reached every level of society.[6]

Other Drugs: Absinthe, Ether and Hashish

remained legal until the early twentieth century, when countries around the world began to realize how damaging they were to health and productivity. Warnings about the dangers of drug use surfaced now and again, and many countries did have laws that restricted drug traffic across borders, but these were in place mainly to collect tax revenues and to protect pharmacists.

Novelists and poets elevated opium in all of its incarnations to the status of a muse, crediting it for releasing

"Haschisch." An article by Francis Carco from the French scandal sheet *Voilà*. Hashish and opium shared the distinction of being exotic drugs. For this article, Carco visited a "fumerie de haschisch" (hashish den) in the Greek port of Piraeus, 4 May 1935.

MARIANI WINE

MARIANI WINE Quickly Restores **HEALTH, STRENGTH, ENERGY & VITALITY.**

MARIANI WINE FORTIFIES, STRENGTHENS, STIMULATES & REFRESHES THE BODY & BRAIN.

HASTENS CONVALESCENCE especially after **INFLUENZA.**

His Holiness **THE POPE** writes that he has greatly appreciated the beneficent effects of this Tonic Wine and has forwarded to Mr. Mariani as a token of gratitude a gold medal bearing his august effigy.

MARIANI WINE

delivered free to all parts of the United Kingdom by WILCOX & CO., 239, Mortimer Street, London, W., price 4/- per Single Bottle, 22 6 half-dozen, 45/- dozen, and is sold by Chemists and Stores.

Mariani Wine. Originally a French product, Mariani Wine, or Vin Mariani as it was known in France, was immensely popular, and advertisements for it appeared regularly in weekly newspapers such as *The Illustrated London News*. According to these ads, *everyone*, including Pope Leo XIII (pictured here) and actress Sarah Bernhardt, were dedicated imbibers of this coca-laced tonic, c. 1898.

them from the tedium of banal thoughts and words. Brilliant writers, able to free themselves from inhibition, shone; dull ones at least had new experiences to write about. Travellers wove opium experiences into their accounts, adding even more spice and danger to already captivating tales.

Looking back at the exuberance of the nineteenth century in industry, art, literature, science, medicine and exploration—all of which advanced at a great pace—it's difficult to see how that era's fascination with intoxicants, stupefiers and narcotics could have hindered progress whatsoever. The spirit of adventure and curiosity that gave the nineteenth-century mind the freedom to experiment with the unknown provoked a reaction that manifested itself in art and literature.

Cinema also exploited the drug craze, with films like *The Derelict* (1914), *The Dividend* (1916), *Broken Blossoms* (1919), *Bits of Life* (1921) and *Human Wreckage* (1924). Rushing in to show the evil influences of "unsavoury" foreign immigrants or the unscrupulous, morphine-wielding medical profession, Hollywood knew it was onto a good thing and cashed in on the box-office draw of drugs.

Even anti-opium crusaders were caught up in the drug's exotic web, revelling in sordid tales of seduction and white slavery, and emphasizing the details that were sure to titillate the public and fuel the flames of their cause. As a consequence, opium smuggling and drug use became favourite themes in detective novels and true crime exposés. Much of the imagery reflects the prejudice and bigotry of the time.

The history of drugs is convoluted, and written references to them are both fascinating and infinite. After a tour of San Francisco's Chinatown, Rudyard Kipling commented that the buildings he saw there were "constructed on the lines of icebergs—two-thirds below sight level."[7] That's precisely what I've discovered about the world of opium: it is rich, complex and pervasive, and this book is but the tip of the iceberg.

The focus here is on the wealth of images and literature celebrating or condemning this fabled drug, and on the writers, artists and photographers who have tried to capture the essence of opium's allure. Whether portraying the atmosphere of Chinatowns in California, the effect of opium on the body or the pleasures of the exotic, the words and pictures produced during the nineteenth century and into the early years of the twentieth reflected the attitudes that guaranteed opium's exalted place in the pantheon of drugs.

The photographs, especially, compel viewers to become voyeurs of a very private history—even when it is obvious they are posed. The waste of time, energy and health is shocking. But still, a part of us envies the ability of opium smokers to commit fully to inertia and pleasure. Above all, we covet their poppied dreams.

This page: Crusaders targeted drug use among young people to get their messages of fear across to the public. They used many platforms, including news reels, magazines and tracts like this one, c.1920, to spread the word. In later decades, "sex-crazed marijuana fiends" became the focus of their campaigns.

Facing page: Race Williams battles drugs, smugglers and a dame named Flame in Carroll John Daly's action-filled adventure, "Just Another Stiff." *Dime Detective Magazine,* April 1936. "Dope! Rivers of it, to flood the nation!"

COMPLETE

10¢ DIME
DETECTIVE
MAGAZINE

MAR 6

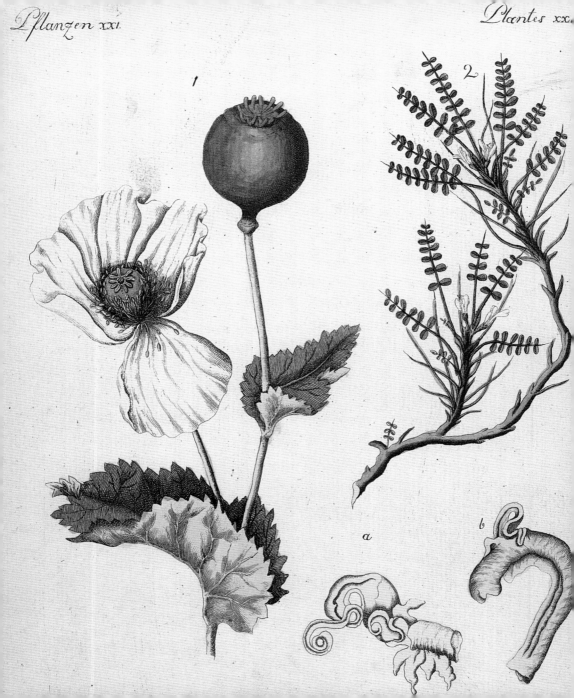

1

2

a

b

THE DROWSY POPPY

"Where would I find opium? The opium that is my life,
the magic opium that intoxicates me with pleasures and
illusions, intrepid opium that here sustains me."

—Claude Farrère, "Hors du silence"[1]

Le Pavot blanc (Opium Poppy). The original caption reads: "The common poppy with white flowers, which supplies us with opium, is frequently cultivated in Germany, but it is only in Turkey, Egypt and Syria that its sap gives us opium." The plant on the left is the opium poppy. The plant on the right is the tragacanth, used by apothecaries for its medicinal gum. Handcoloured copperplate engraving from *Porte-feuille des enfans,* vol. I, no. 99, by Charles Frédéric, 1795.

The opium poppy, *Papaver somniferum*—the poppy that brings sleep, the source of the "drowsy syrup" in Shakespeare's *Othello*—is the beautiful flower that answers Farrère's desperate question of where to find his precious opium.

There are almost a hundred different kinds of poppies, but only the *Papaver somniferum* produces opium in sufficient quantity that long made it an important part of the *materia medica,* or medicines, of Europe, the Middle East, India and China.

The opium poppy is an annual belonging to the family Papaveraceæ (order Papaverales).[2] Within the species are many varieties, distinguished by petal and seed colour, and by number of petals. In general they grow to a

Poppy Song

O poppy-buds, that in the golden air

Wave heavy hanging censers of delight,

Give me an anodyne for my despair;

O crimson poppy-blooms, O golden blight,

O careless drunken heavy poppy-flowers,

Make that the day for me be as the night.

Give me to lie down in your drowsy bowers,

That having breathed of your rich perfume,

My soul may have all-rest through all the hours;

So shall I lie within my little room.

While the poor tyrants of the world go by,

Restfully shrouded in your velvet gloom,

Beneath the wide face of the cloudless sky.

—Park Barnitz, *The Book of Jade*³

Poppy Medicine

Less effective than opium were medicines such as Meconium (from the Greek word *mekon*) and Diacodium, which were made from decocting poppy heads and leaves. Other medicines such as Theriac and Mithridate, were complex concoctions composed of up to seventy-five ingredients, often including opium. Produced as early as the first century B.C., they were alternately praised or scorned. Theriac, which was known in Britain and America as Venice Treacle, was used right up into the nineteenth century.[6]

The opium poppy. From *The Family Physician*, c. 1900.

height of three to four feet, the stem is cylindrical and solid, and the roots are thick and tapering. The buds droop, but when in flower the plant stands erect. *Papaver somniferum* usually has white or purple flowers with four large concave petals, and the capsules are globe shaped, containing a central cavity partially separated by papery dividers and filled with pale yellow seeds.[4] The potency of the opium depends on the growing conditions.

The word "opium" comes from the Greek οποσ or *opos* (juice), and οπιον or *opion* (poppy juice), and it is likely that the poppy plant itself originated in the Mediterranean area. The ancient Greeks called the opium poppy plant μακϖν or *mekon*. The Peloponnesian town of Sikyon was formerly named Mekone, or Poppy Town.[5]

The beginnings of opium use go so far back that they are lost in history. There's little doubt, however, that the poppy was used and traded for millennia throughout the Mediterranean, the Middle East, Asia Minor and Western Europe as a multipurpose plant, supplying food, animal fodder, oil and fuel. Less certain is how early it was recognized for its narcotic or medicinal properties. Enthusiastic claims have been made asserting that the plant played an important part in rituals and medical treatment as far back as the third millennium B.C., but scholarly re-evaluation of written and pictorial evidence from prehistoric and early historic sites in Assyria, Mycenæ and Egypt has shown some of these conclusions to be premature.

In Roman times, Ovid wrote the poem "Cosmetics for Ladies" about the poppy as a beauty product, although he wasn't specific about its properties:

> *"I've seen a girl soak poppies in cold water,*
> *Pound them and rub them on her tender cheeks."*[7]

Pavot (Poppy). The original caption reads: "The poppy flower, sumptuous and heavy, secretes the liquor which brings sleep and dreams, but which kills more surely than the most deadly epidemics." From *Lectures pour tous*, 1899, p. 504.

Early references to poppies may have had more to do with the plant's image as a symbol of fertility than its use as a drug. Mark David Merlin, author of *On the Trail of the Ancient Opium Poppy*, quotes a report that the taxonomist Linnæus once counted the number of seeds in a single poppy capsule. The resulting total of 32,000 seeds may have been a bit on the high side, but it does illustrate the poppy's showy fecundity.[8]

The debate over the historic use of opium includes a passage from Homer's *Odyssey*. Helen of Troy spikes some wine with *nepenthes*, "a drug that had the power of robbing grief and anger of their sting and banishing all painful memories," in order to help friends forget Odysseus' disappearance. Nepenthes may have been opium or cannabis or a mixture of drugs. The physician Dioscorides (first century A.D.) guessed that it was a compound of ingredients that included opium and henbane.★[9]

★ Henbane *(Hyoscyamus niger)* is a potent painkiller with a justifiably bad reputation: it's also extremely poisonous.

Morpheus

Often presented as evidence of early recognition of the poppy's soporific qualities is the existence of the Greek god Morpheus, variously called the god of sleep or of dreams. It is likely, however, that Morpheus was unknown to the ancient Greeks, and first appeared as a creation of the Roman poet Ovid (43 B.C.–c. A.D. 17). In *Metamorphoses*, Ovid wrote that of the thousand sons of Somnos, the god of sleep, Morpheus was the only one capable of taking on human form.[10]

However, by Dioscorides' time the use of opium as a soporific was certainly known, and Ovid alludes to it in *Fasti,* writing: "Her calm brow wreathed with poppies, / Night drew on, and in her train brought darkling dreams." Another Roman poet, Virgil, wrote in *The Æneid:* "The dragon, guarding well the holy boughs / With honey dripping slow and drowsy poppy."[11]

$$C_{17}H_{19}O_3N$$

Morphine's molecular formula (above): carbon, hydrogen, oxygen and nitrogen.

The chemical structures of the morphine alkaloid (background, top) and heroin, a chemical synthesis of morphine (background, bottom). The alkaloids codeine, papaverine, narcotine, narceine and thebaine, among others, are also found in opium. Other naturally occurring alkaloids used as drugs include atropine, from belladonna; cocaine, from the coca leaf; mescaline, from peyote; and nicotine, from tobacco.

The poppy's magic comes from morphine, the principal active ingredient in opium. Morphine is an alkaloid, an organic compound, many of which have toxic, stimulant or analgesic effects. Friedrich Wilhelm Sertürner isolated morphine and published his results in 1805, describing the substance as the *Principium Somniferum,* or the sleepmaking principle, and naming it *Morphium.*[12] Of the thirty or so other alkaloids in opium, codeine is the most important.

Morphine, pure and strong unlike raw opium,★ burst onto the drug scene on the heels of the invention of the functional hypodermic needle by Dr. Alexander Wood in 1853.[13] Although morphine could be taken orally, experimenters noticed that the response to injecting it under the skin was far more rapid.

As narcotics, opium, morphine and heroin are drugs that relieve pain, relax spasms, reduce fevers and induce sleep. Acting as an analgesic, or pain reliever, the morphine

★ Raw opium has a morphine content that ranges from 3 to 20 per cent, depending on where it has been cultivated and how it has been processed.

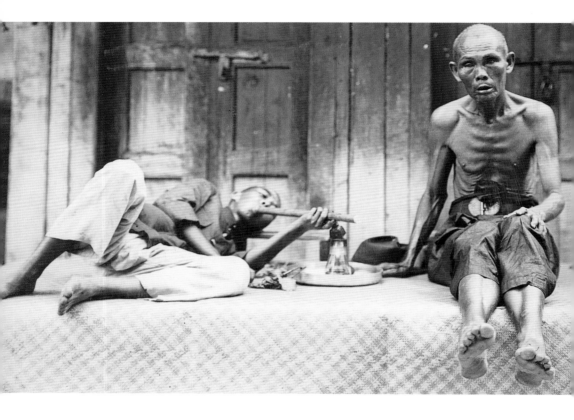

"Smokers while asleep are like corpses, lean and haggard as demons. Opium-smoking throws whole families into ruin, dissipates every kind of property, and ruins man himself . . . It wastes the flesh and blood until the skin hangs down in bags and their bones are as naked as billets of wood. When the smoker has pawned everything in his possession, he will pawn his wife and sell his daughters."—John Thomson, The Land and the People of China[14]

blocks messages of pain to the brain, producing euphoria and deadening anxieties and tensions.[15] It also suppresses coughs, constipates by inhibiting the flow of gastric juices, slows down respiration and dilates the blood vessels in the skin. All of these characteristics are invaluable in medicine, not to cure specific illnesses or injuries but to provide relief from symptoms. Taken in the wrong quantities, however, the relief can turn injurious or fatal.

Heroin, a semi-synthetic substance derived from morphine by simple structural modification, was first created in the 1870s, shelved, and then rediscovered in 1898 by Heinrich Dreser, a chemist for the Bayer Company of Germany.[16] Heroin was initially marketed as a remedy for tuberculosis, laryngitis and coughs. It was also, ironically, touted as a potential cure for morphine addiction.

The cultivation of poppies, the collection of the sap and the transformation of the sap into raw opium was long and complicated. Essentially the same in India, Turkey, Persia and China—although specifics varied from one area to the other—the process defied mechanization, changing little through the centuries. Poppies continue to be cultivated today, just as opium continues to be harvested, but the description given here—using the Indian model—is in the past tense because many details involving trade and quantities no longer exist.

In India, opium production was concentrated in the Ganges regions of Benares and Behar, and farther west in

Chinese opium smokers in Southeast Asia. The emaciated state of the smoker on the right may have been due to causes other than opium dependency, but his malnourished body conforms with the accounts of travellers who visited Chinese opium dens in the nineteenth century, c. 1930.

the province of Malwa. Poppies were sown in November and required intensive irrigation throughout the three-month growing period. When the petals were dropping off and the capsules had swelled, they were ready to be harvested.

First, workers removed and set aside all remaining poppy petals. At sunrise, harvesters incised the pods vertically with a 3- to 4-blade tool called a *nushtur*, taking care not to cut into the capsule. The next morning the exuded sap was collected, drained and then air dried for about a month, before being sent to government factories to be tested for water content and purity and to be prepared for sale.

Rudyard Kipling was overwhelmed by the bureaucracy of the factory in Ghazipur, the opium capital of Benares. "Never was such a place for forms," he quipped,[17] then added, "No one trusts any one in Ghazipur. They are always weighing, testing, and assaying."[18]

The dried opium, divided by grade, was tossed into tanks and kneaded by men treading the mass. Opium for the domestic market was formed into cakes and wrapped in oiled paper; opium for export was rolled into small balls and pressed into bowls lined with a layer of the petals that had been collected earlier. These balls were covered and stuck together with *lewa,* the liquid that had been drained

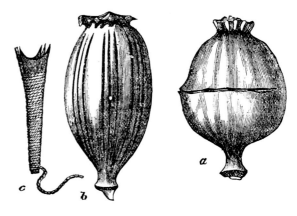

A nushtur or incisor (c), a poppy pod showing the vertical cuts made by harvesters in India (b), and another with a horizontal cut that would be made in Turkey (a). A *seetoah* or scraper was used to remove the exuded sap. Opium from a single poppy could be harvested several times over a period of days. From the *Encyclopædia Britannica*, 1884, p. 812.

Fertile Poppy Fields

In 1883 there were 876,454 acres under poppy cultivation in Behar and Benares alone, much of it on the rich Ganges plain. Farmers who grew poppies were obliged to sell their crops to the government at a fixed price (about 30 per cent of what the government could sell it for).[23]

"Indian Coolies Going to the Poppy-Fields." *Knox's Boy Travellers* (1881) follows the adventures of Frank and Fred around the world. They arrived in the Ganges region in November, just as the poppies were about to be sown, p. 351.

from the opium. When the balls were removed from the bowls, they were covered with "poppy trash"—powdered leaves, capsules and stems—and then were stored in a dry place until ready to be packed into chests. About forty balls fit into each chest.[19]

The opium was put on sale at auction in October, almost a year after the seeds were first sown. Kipling was told that at the height of the season, Ghazipur held, in its numerous and immense storehouses, some £3,500,000 worth of opium.[20]

Because opium was sold by weight, the purchasers had to guard against adulteration by substances such as sand, lead, mud, sugar, molasses and cow dung. Historian S. Wells Williams wrote that pure opium cut cleanly without leaving shreds along the edge; when spread thinly onto a flat surface it appeared translucent, had a "gallstone yellow" colour and a granular texture; the mass was sticky and "tremulous like strawberry jam."[21]

In India alone, the annual income produced from sales of opium, not even accounting for inflation, was staggering. Opium brought in £750,000 in 1840 but by 1878 was bringing in £9,100,000; the total revenue over 39 years was £375,000,000. On the other hand, expenses related to opium for 1876 and '77 were a paltry £2,841,647.[22]

The Business of Opium

The number of workers and officials involved in processing opium meant that cities like Ghazipur and Patna were beehives of activity during harvest and production. Kipling wrote in his book *From Sea to Sea* (1910) that Ghazipur alone employed some 250 workers. Officials claimed that each worker could turn out one cake of opium every four minutes.[24]

"The Indo-Chinese Opium Trade: Notes at an Opium Factory at Patna." These three illustrations, chosen from an original series of six, are remarkable for their depiction of the magnitude of the opium-manufacturing industry in India. *Far left:* "The Drying Room"; *this page, top:* "The Balling Room"; *this page, bottom:* "The Stacking Room." Engraved from drawings by Lieut.-Colonel Walter S. Sherwill, *The Graphic,* 24 June 1882, p. 640.

The purchaser of raw opium looked for the following characteristics: "Moderately firm texture, capable of receiving an impression from the finger; of a dark yellow color when held in the light, but nearly black in the mass, with a strong smell, and free from grittiness."—"Articles of Import and Export of Canton," *The Chinese Repository* [25]

River Scene on the Hooghly, Calcutta.

This page: "River Scene on the Hooghly, Calcutta." Packed chests of opium were taken to auction—Patna and Ghazipur opium went to Calcutta, and Malwa opium to Bombay—where the only restriction on purchase was the ability of the bidder to pay. Once bought, the opium would be shipped to its destination from ports such as this one. Postcard, c. 1911.

Facing page: "Opium Merchant." This woodcut from *Knox's Boy Travellers* (1881) was accompanied by a detailed description of how the poppy was cultivated, along with a fierce invective against the English for their involvement in the opium trade, p. 353.

In 1909 the curious traveller could consult *Murray's Handbook to India, Burma & Ceylon* for information about opium cultivation and exportation or visit the Indore opium market in the Haldi Bazaar near the Sharafa Street money lenders.[26] *Murray's Handbook,* however, didn't advise tourists on where to go to smoke it.

India didn't have a monopoly on opium production, although it was the main source of smoking opium for the Chinese. Turkey, Persia (Iran) and China also produced opium, as did Greece, Bulgaria, Yugoslavia and Egypt. For domestic use in medicines such as laudanum and Dover's Powder, the British bought Turkish opium because of its reliability and high morphine count of 10 to 13 per cent.

Each area packaged its opium differently: Turkey produced small cakes (wrapped in poppy leaves) called "Constantinople pats"; Persia made six-inch-long cylindrical sticks like incense known as "Trebizond"; and China offered white paper-wrapped flat cakes called "Yunnan."[27]

The Turks, who called opium by the Arabic word *afion* or *afyun,* had a notorious reputation for opium consumption. Robert Burton, the author of *The Anatomy of Melancholy* (1621), quoted the traveller Garcias ab Horto, who wrote that some Turks take opium to "helpeth digestions, and procureth alacrity." Pierre Pomet, the author of *A Compleat History of Druggs* (1694), claimed that, before battle, Turkish soldiers would take opium "to excess, that it may animate them, or at least make them insensible of Danger." The well-travelled Italian, Edmondo de Amicis, wrote in *Constantinople* (1896), that, to the Turks, coffee, opium, wine and tobacco were "pleasure's couches."[28]

French writer Théophile Gautier described the intoxicating Turkish bazaars in his book *Constantinople* (1857):

There, exposed in heaps or in open bags, were henna, sandalwood, antimony, powdered dyes, dates, cinnamon, benzoin [a resin used in perfumes], pistachios, amber, mastic, ginger, nutmeg, opium, hashish, all guarded by nonchalant merchants who sat with legs crossed and who seemed benumbed by this perfume saturated air.[29]

Above: "Types of Turkish Soldiers." European authors delighted in spreading wild and inflammatory claims about the prowess and courage of Turkish soldiers under the influence of opium. From Edmondo de Amicis, *Constantinople,* 1896, facing p. 189. Photogravure by W. H. Gilbo.

Left, background: Afion (afyun), the Arabic word for opium.

"The Drug Bazaar." *The Illustrated London News* called this bazaar the most picturesque of Constantinople's many markets. 15 October 1853, p. 321.

No matter where poppies were grown, and in spite of the labour-intensive nature of cultivation, harvesting and production, entrepreneurs recognized the potential for astounding profits, especially in those countries where the workforce came cheap. This exploitation led to a lucrative and unethical industry that relied on greed and human weakness for its success.

Chandu

The Ghazipur balls and Patna cakes of raw opium from India were delivered throughout Asia to establishments that were responsible for turning them into *chandu,* or smoking opium. In Singapore, Java and Indochina, these were government-licensed monopolies known by the misleading name of "opium farms."[30] Their intricate and painstaking process turned the raw opium into the desired consistency for smoking, eliminated impurities such as vegetable matter, and removed harsh oils and resins.

Workers broke the opium balls in half and scooped out the gelatinous mass within. The outer shells were boiled and all the opium from them extracted through a repeated process of filtering through paper. This extracted opium was mixed with the gelatinous stuff already removed from the core of the shell.

Preparing opium for smoking. *This page, top:* breaking open the balls of opium; *bottom:* kneading the paste.

Next, the raw opium was heated and reduced to the consistency of treacle (molasses). Then, in a series of repeated steps, it was boiled, spread out, boiled again, and so on, until it reached a satisfactory consistency.

The workers put this paste into bowls, kneaded it and spread it out in shallow pans. The paste was heated evenly, turned over and over, and exposed directly to the heat until it was properly coloured and, once again, of the right consistency. The resulting flat cakes were stacked in vats of water and boiled until they dissolved. This liquid was filtered, reduced over a fire, then whipped up like egg whites to introduce microbes that hastened fermentation. Journalist Fernand Honoré wrote that it had a "very fine aroma, but one not easily defined . . . [it reminds] one of well-ripened pomegranates quickly followed by the scent of poppy seeds at harvest time."[31]

The resulting chandu was packaged and sold throughout Asia.

CHINA

BY W. HUGHES

Towns of the 1st Class (foo) are written thus . Han-yang
do . 2nd do. (choo) . do. . Loun-gan
do . 3rd do. (hien) and all others
are of smaller size, as .

The Coast-line is copied from the Charts recently
published at the Admiralty, London; the Lol-Choo
from a survey executed by the British Officers in
1845, & supplied by the kindness of Captain Beau-
fort, R.N. The other parts are chiefly from the
Jesuits' great Map.

The five ports opened to commerce by
the Treaty of this year (1842) are Canton,
Amoy, Fuh-choo, Ning-po, and Shang-
hae, or Ching-hae, (in Kiang-su province).

English Miles 69=One Degree

Geographical Miles 60=One Degree

W Hughes

On the same scale as Chusan

English Miles

OPIUM AND THE EAST

"Il parlait lentement des voyages en Chine,
*Des mandarins fumant les pipes de bambou."**

—Maurice Magre, "L'Officier de marine"[1]

By the late fifteenth century, medieval Europeans had acquired tastes or needs for many scarce and precious products from the Far East, and opium was one of these, thanks to Arab traders who helped spread its medicinal use, not only into southern Europe, by way of Spain, but also into North Africa, India and China.

Up until this time, trade with the Levant, the countries of the Eastern Mediterranean, which had received goods from India and China largely via coastal sea routes, satisfied the demand for opium and for the pepper, silks, spices, herbs and tea of Asia. But to bypass the slowness and uncertainty of the transactions and to eliminate the

Map of China. Based on survey information gathered in 1842 by the British Royal Navy (the coast) and the "Jesuit's great map" (the interior). By W. Hughes, published by A. & C. Black, Edinburgh, 1851. The names of the five treaty ports opened to British traders in 1842— Canton, Shanghai (Shang-hae), Amoy, Foochow (Fuh-choo) and Ningpo (Ning-po)—are underscored in red.

---

* He spoke slowly of his voyages to China,
  And of the mandarins who smoked their pipes of bamboo.

The Zamorin of Calicut granting
de Gama Audience.

G. Shea. sc.

"The Zamorin of Calicut granting [Vasco] de [*sic*] Gama Audience." Copperplate engraving by G. Shea from an unidentified book, c. 1820.

Duarte Barbosa

Duarte Barbosa, a Portuguese civil servant employed in India from about 1500 to 1516, wrote an account of his voyage to India. Barbosa filled his pages with details of the customs, produce and trade items at each of his stops, noting that the Arabian traders particularly dealt in cotton, rhubarb, pearls, precious metals, jewels, ivory, slaves, silk, honey, spices and drugs, including opium.[2]

LORD CLIVE.

Sir Robert Clive (1725–74), British general and founder of Britain's Indian Empire. He developed a severe addiction to laudanum in an effort to stave off headaches and chest pains.[5] Opium use was common among Europeans living in India; it was one of the few medicines that could allay the fevers and diarrhœa of cholera and dysentery. Engraving by Henry Wallis, undated.

middlemen, European explorers set out to find their own routes to the sources of these wonderful goods.

One of first, the Portuguese explorer Vasco da Gama, sailed around the Cape of Good Hope and reached the port of Calicut on the Malabar Coast in 1498. Managing to get on good terms with the *zamorin,* the European name for the local rajah, he established a trade monopoly with India that lasted until 1600. Portugal's hold was challenged by Holland, France and especially Britain, whose soldiers and statesmen—such as the legendary Sir Robert Clive—ensured its rise to power during the next two centuries. The British defeated their rivals in a number of clashes and were granted concessions by Indian rulers on the cultivation and export of opium, which was quickly becoming an important trade item with the Chinese.[3]

In the meantime, the Portuguese had established a trade monopoly with the Chinese in 1557, using Macao as their centre. When this monopoly was dissolved in 1685, opportunities opened up for the British, Dutch and other nations that had been trying to establish a foothold since the early seventeenth century. Again, Britain defeated its European rivals and by 1715 had become the principal agency in Canton, the only Chinese port open for trade.[4]

The Chinese were, by this time, already trying to eradicate the opium vice from their shores.

Opium had been introduced to China as a medicinal trade item by the Arabs during the eighth-century T'ang dynasty, or perhaps even a century before.[6]

J. Edkins made a relatively thorough study of the beginnings of opium use in *Opium: Historical Note* (1898). He quoted numerous early poems about the poppy's qualities, including a tenth-century one that declared the poppy could be made into a drink "fit for Buddha." A twelfth-century medical treatise praised the poppy's effect against dysentery as "magical."[7]

According to Margaret Goldsmith, author of *The Trail of Opium* (1939), the first written description of opium smoking appears in a 1746 pamphlet. Huang Yu-pu, a government investigator, noted that opium from Java was smoked mixed with tobacco, which had been introduced by the Spanish 150 years before. But Edkins, who also refers to this account, reports that Kæmpfer, the author of *Amœnitates exoticæ* (1712), had observed the practice years earlier in 1689 in Batavia (Java), where water-diluted opium was smoked with tobacco. By 1729 the vice had spread enough to disturb the Chinese Emperor Yung Ching, who prohibited both opium-smoking houses and the sale of opium.[8]

By 1767 the trading of Malwa opium by the Portuguese to the Chinese had become notable.[9] The

The Eight Regulations

Emperor K'ang Hsi (early eighteenth century) set conditions for European traders. Warships were prohibited from entering the Pearl River; arms, wives or families were not allowed in Canton nor could trade take place outside winter months. Chinese employed by foreigners required licenses and the number of servants was limited. Sedan chairs, boating for pleasure and excursions into the city were forbidden, except for 3 visits a month to the Honan Island public gardens if the visitors limited their numbers to 10 and did not get drunk or mingle. Business had to be conducted through the Hong merchants, and ships were to load at Whampoa. Finally, there was to be no smuggling and no credit.[10]

"Chinese Smoking Opium." The two seated figures in the foreground are smoking tobacco. Lithograph from *China and Japan*, 1870, by James B. Lawrence, faces p. 239.

Oh! Monstrous Folly!

Chinese proclamations and edicts against opium were issued frequently. This is an example from 1839: "Oh! monstrous folly! Oh! stupidity unparalleled! Ye aim after profit, but to make profit is impossible: ye try to preserve your lives, but even to do that is equally difficult! Ye take your money and purchase *death!*" [13]

Facing page and this page, background: Yen-kau and Ya-pien-yen, the Chinese symbols for smoking opium. Ya-pien is the Chinese word for opium. From J. Edkins, Opium: Historical Note, p. v.

British may have begun exporting small shipments to China by this time [11] but were definitely established by 1773 and then semi–officially by 1780, thanks to the East India Company's monopoly on the selling of opium in India. Opium represented huge profits not only for the East India Company, but an ongoing prosperity for almost all those involved in the drug trade between Britain, India and China.

Chinese connoisseurs reportedly preferred the taste of opium from India, particularly Benares, to that from Turkey, Persia and especially China. Père M. Huc, a missionary and traveller to China in the mid–nineteenth century, contradicted this; he alleged that opium from India was so badly adulterated once it reached China that it could not compete in quality with the Chinese product. He also claimed that since Indian opium was priced considerably higher, it was attractive to vain smokers who wanted to show off their wealth. [12] Perhaps the cynical observations of Chinese cabinet minister Chu Tsun were closer to the truth. He

declared that the local product could never succeed as it would never be as well made, and furthermore, "All men prize what is strange and undervalue whatever is in ordinary use."[14]

The disdain for locally grown opium ensured a market for the imported stuff. But, even though access to trade with the Chinese had been briefly unrestricted, by the first half of the nineteenth century the only port available to the traders was Canton, a city of immense importance. It was, in fact, illegal to offload opium in Canton, but this became a mere technicality to both the sellers and the buyers.

Foreign traders were quite aware that they were breaking the laws of China by bringing opium into the country, but the British government, at least, could soothe its conscience knowing that the trade was conducted several steps removed through the East India Company and even more distantly through private traders.

The problem with China was that it didn't really want the goods offered by Britain, the United States and European nations in exchange for its badly needed tea, silk and rhubarb.★ So the British, in an effort to maintain

★ Rhubarb was commonly used by Europeans as a laxative and was an important trade item. They purchased so much that the Chinese believed that if it were withheld from them, they would die of constipation.[15]

Above: Le Comprador chinois (The Chinese Compradore). Saigon, c. 1906.

Facing page: "Opium-Smoker's Progress—Past, Present, Future." A cautionary tale against the use of opium. The smoker faces a future of destitution. From W. A. P. Martin's *A Cycle of Cathay,* 1896, p. 87.

The Hoppo

The Chinese official known as the "Hoppo" was glorified in a 1753 publication called *The Hoppo Book,* by an unnamed trader. It outlined Canton trade regulations and taxes payable on items such as opium, sugar, tea and musk. That the long-forbidden opium was mentioned wasn't the only surprise; it was listed at only a half ounce of silver per catty (about ¾ lb.), far cheaper than many of the other items.[18]

OPIUM-SMOKER'S PROGRESS—PAST, PRESENT, FUTURE.

a trade balance, focussed on the lucrative sale of contraband opium, offloading it in isolated spots, or more openly on the island of Lintin, near Canton. The Chinese themselves also took an energetic role, accepting bribes and cultivating poppies. China's large population and long-established familiarity with opium guaranteed a strong market for the drug; it was only necessary for European traders to import it in sufficient quantities and cheaply enough to encourage addiction.

As far as legitimate trade was concerned, the foreigners had to conduct business with Hong, or Co-Hong, merchants, a monopoly of Chinese middlemen who were ultimately responsible for the trader's conduct. But trade wasn't a simple matter of just sitting down and striking a bargain. The foreigners also needed *compradores,* their own agents, who could be trusted to represent them. The Hong merchants, in turn, were obliged to deal with an emperor-appointed official known as the Hai Kwan Pu (vulgarized by the foreigners as the "Hoppo"). Unofficial brokers, known as "melters," facilitated sales of illegal opium.[16]

Each level of this bureaucracy had to pay huge sums for the privilege of trading, on top of donations, commissions and gifts. Hong merchants were required to post bonds guaranteeing that ships unloading at Whampoa did not carry opium, but this was blatantly overlooked through widespread bribery.[17]

Above: "The European Factories, Canton." From *The Chinese Empire* by George N. Wright, 1858. Steelplate engraving by J. Tingle, based on a drawing by Thomas Allom.

Facing page: Canton, 1857. From Charles H. Eden's *China: Historical and Descriptive,* 1877, p. 90.

Canton

In the 1830s and '40s, the heyday of the opium trade, Canton's waterfront was a lively place, swarming with lorchas and junks (two types of small Chinese trading ships), delivering goods to the "factories," as the foreigners' warehouses were called.[19]

Located up a tortuous serpentine channel called The Bogue, Canton, the capital of the province of Kwangtung, was well protected, although not invincible. Whampoa, where the unloading of ships took place, was one of the many islands that packed The Bogue. From there, the goods would be transported to Canton through maritime traffic jams of fishing boats, fruit, flower, duck, barber and brothel boats; and houseboats and passenger boats.[20]

Encircled by thirty-foot walls, Canton hid all but its port from the voyager arriving by sea. The wharves, lined with the factories of English, American, Parsee, Swedish, Spanish, French and Danish traders, not to mention the Chinese, were isolated from the city proper. The factories were quite large and self-contained; Britain's featured offices, storerooms, apartments, a treasury, a garden and a church.[21]

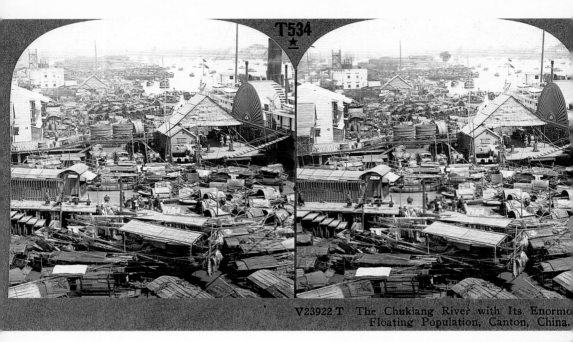

V23922 T The Chukiang River with Its Enormo
Floating Population, Canton, China.

Canton

According to author Maurice Collis, who sketched a vivid picture of Canton in *Foreign Mud,* the square that separated the factories from the river was one of the few places where a merchant could stretch his legs in the otherwise forbidden city. It bustled with constant activity: "Pedlars, hawkers, peep-show men and loungers, cobblers, tailors, and sellers of tea or nuts, not to speak of men who just stared or begged loudly, packed this little promenade." [22]

CANTO

Facing page: View of the harbour at Canton. From a stereocard, c. 1900.

Right: A street in Canton. From Ridpath's *History of the World*, vol. 4, 1899, p. 807. Credited to Howland.

Below: The European, Indian and American factories of Canton, as seen from the water. From Fitch W. Taylor's *A Voyage Round the World,* 1842, p. 139. Taylor visited Canton in 1839, just before hostilities reached their peak.

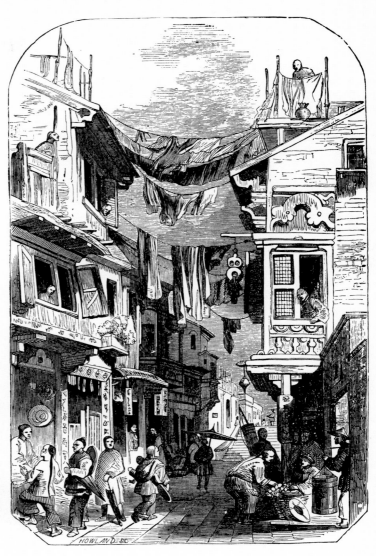

Foreigners were not the only ones involved in smuggling, according to the 1832 *Chinese Repository*: "OPIUM—When governor Le visited Peking last year, his son took with him a quantity of opium, some thousands of dollars' worth, to give away to the great men about the court. As a governor's baggage is not searched there was no fear of detection. The opium dealer who supplied his excellency's son with the drug, cheated him by putting up one half of it of a very bad quality. On the governor's return, it was his intention to punish the offender, not for putting up bad opium, but for dealing in it at all . . . The culprit heard what was coming, and absconded with the fruit of his fraud."[23]

Chinese edicts not only opposing the importation of opium but limiting all trade had been proliferating since the early eighteenth century, but that did not stop traders from evading the laws by bribery, by shipping to other ports or by smuggling.

Facing page: Contrebandiers d'opium saisis par la police chinoise (Opium Smugglers Captured by Chinese Police). Engraving from an unidentified French illustrated paper, c. 1850.

This page: "An Unfortunate Thief." He's wearing the collar, or cangue, a once common means of punishment in China. Based on a photograph by John Thomson from Dix ans de voyage dans la Chine et l'Indo-Chine (Illustrations of China and Its People), 1877.

A Singular Punishment

Smokers *were* eventually targeted, as this note from the 1838 *Chinese Repository* shows: "Opium, opium dealers and smokers, with their apparatus for smoking, have been recently seized . . . and, if report be true, the singular punishment of cutting out a portion of the upper lip, to prevent smoking, has been resorted to in Hoopih."[26]

Laws for foreigners were rarely enforced; it was considered preferable to punish locals who co-operated with them. These laws were haphazardly applied but penalties were severe: sellers could be banished or forced to wear a wooden collar, den keepers could be strangled. Oddly, though, for a time at least, smokers themselves were exempt; perhaps, speculated Edkins, it was thought that as slaves to this revolting habit they were already suffering punishment.[24]

Supplying an illegal commodity like opium must have required a fair bit of self-justification on the part of the European officials and traders. Many were God-fearing men who would have been horrified to promote the addictive substance in their own countries. One unidentified Englishman's rationale, that opium was just "a harmless luxury," that the economy benefited from the solace provided to the ever-productive Chinese and, as a last gasp, that if the opium trade were in less respectable hands it would land in the laps of "desperadoes, pirates, and marauders," was even echoed by those not involved in the trade.[25]

Opium Clippers

The merchants who bought the opium in India—large companies like Jardine, Matheson or individuals just trying to make an easy fortune—needed to get it to China as quickly as possible, in order to recoup the costs and to avoid the dangers of storms and pirates on the China coast. To this end a new kind of ship was designed: the sleek, fast opium clipper.

These clippers offloaded at Lintin, or in isolated harbours and creeks, trading their contraband for silver in secrecy. Silver was acceptable in any form, as long as it could be weighed; bars, antiques, bits of cutlery, all were accepted as legal tender. The heavy outflow of silver threatened economic hardship for China but meant heady profits for the traders.[27]

Above: "Opium Clipper, *Ly-ee-moon*."
Built by the Thames Shipbuilding Corp.
for Messrs. Dent of Hong Kong, the
Ly-ee-moon weighed 1001 tons, was
270 feet long, 27 feet wide and could
travel nearly 17 knots, fast for the time.
The Illustrated London News, 14 July
1860, p. 37.

Left: The Eamont. This 200-ton opium
clipper sailed the China Seas from Hong
Kong to Formosa in the 1850s.
Uncredited line drawing from *A Cruise
in an Opium Clipper* by Lindsay
Anderson, 1891.

To suppress the opium trade, the emperor appointed Lin Tse-haü, Commissioner Lin,★ and bestowed upon him broad powers. Arriving in Canton in March 1839, Lin demanded the surrender of all the opium in the traders' possession as well as guarantees that they would cease shipping it. The merchants agreed to hand over a certain amount—but not all—of the opium. Unimpressed, Lin told them it wasn't enough.[28]

More opium was given up: 22,283 chests valued at about $9 million. Starting on 3 June 1839 at the village of Chunhow, the surrendered opium, mixed with lime, was poured into a creek that fed into the bay. Lin also destroyed opium and opium pipes turned in by Chinese merchants, along with the year's domestic poppy crop.[29]

Continued ship seizures, misunderstandings, discontent and ultimatums eventually led to war. The first Opium War, between China, Britain and other nations, was provoked by the traders' refusal to stop shipping opium to China, and lasted from 1839 until the signing of the Treaty of Nanking in 1842.

★ A wax effigy of Commissioner Lin, along with his favourite consort, was featured in an exhibition at Madame Tussaud's in London in 1846.[30]

Queen Victoria

In preparation for war, Commissioner Lin of China assembled troops and wrote to Queen Victoria, pointing out the evils of the opium trade. A draft of his highly moral letter was published in the May 1839 *Chinese Repository* but probably not sent. His second, less poetic version, was sent in January 1840, but there is no record of the Queen ever having received it.[31]

Left: Queen Victoria, two years before Commissioner Lin thought of writing to her. From Sarah Tyler's *Life of Her Most Gracious Majesty The Queen,* c. 1898. Steelplate engraving by H. Robinson from a miniature by R. Thorburn.

Right: "Bombardment of Canton by the English." From Ridpath's *History of the World,* vol. 4, 1899, p. 810.

How long does it take to destroy opium?

With 500 men, destroying nearly 1,300 chests a day, Lin calculated that he'd need 18 days; he finished in 23. The 22,283 chests each contained about 160 lbs. of opium, making a total of 3,565,280 lbs.[33]

"Looking at the war, therefore, as growing out of [the opium] trade, and waged to recover the losses, . . . it was an unjust one. It was, moreover, an immoral contest . . . and the fact could not be concealed that Great Britain, the first Christian power, really waged this war against the pagan monarch who had vainly endeavored to put down a vice hurtful to his people."—S. Wells Williams, *The Middle Kingdom*[32]

The treaty forced the Chinese to reopen the port of Canton; open the additional ports of Amoy, Shanghai, Foochow and Ningpo to British traders and officials; cede Hong Kong to Britain; and reimburse and pay a heavy compensation of almost $20 million.[34]

The opium trade resumed, once again illegally, under a liberal misinterpretation of the treaty, which at no point had specified that opium would become legal. By 1856, with piracy, opium smuggling and addiction at an all-time high, the Chinese were again desperate to end the trade. The second Opium War, declared by the British, who were joined by the French, ended with another defeat for China. In 1858, the Treaty of Tientsin gave the foreigners even more freedom and power and, though not specified in so many words, ostensibly legalized trade in opium.[35] From this point on, the quantities of opium brought into China exploded. The flooding of the market accelerated its use and, subsequently, levels of addiction grew ever higher.

Chinese domestic opium crop production, earlier a fledgling industry, began to take itself seriously; Baron Richthofen, on a survey of China, wrote in 1872 that several Chinese states had started exporting, importing and bartering opium amongst themselves, notably the provinces of Shensi,★ Shansi, Kansu, Honan, Yünnan and Sz'-chwan.[36]

The years following the second Opium War saw a great increase in the European population in Asia. Naval officers and sailors from the West became a common

The Cost of War

Winning the two Opium Wars was not without its price. In 1860, *The Illustrated London News* reported that the first war cost the British Government £3,500,000 and the East India Company £1,000,000; the second cost a total of £5,400,000.[37]

Rejected by the Army

In 1832, *The Chinese Repository* reported: "Of a thousand men sent by the governor of Canton . . . the commanding officer has sent back two hundred, rendered totally unfit for active service, by the habit of opium-smoking."[38]

★ Opium Maxim

"Out of ten Shen-si people, eleven smokers."[39]

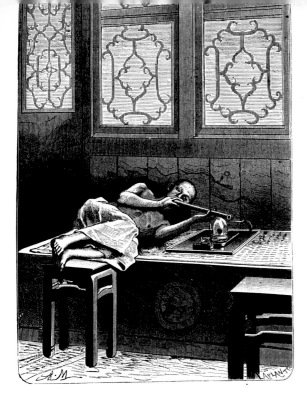

Fumeur d'opium (Opium Smoker). This woodcut, based on a photograph by John Thomson, appeared in the 1877 Hachette edition of Thomson's *Dix ans de voyage dans la Chine et l'Indo-Chine* (*Illustrations of China and Its People*). Hachette reused the image in Léon Rousset's *À Travers la Chine*, 1886. Engraving by Charles Laplante.

sight on the docks and back streets of Canton, as well as in the recently opened port of Shanghai, Britain's new territory of Hong Kong, and Saigon, the capital of France's colony, Indochina. Both American and British Christian missionaries descended in large numbers to spread the Gospel throughout Asia. Tourists, military personnel and businessmen passed through more frequently; entrepreneurs, diplomats and their families took up residence.

A great many of these travellers, missionaries and diplomats published accounts of their visits, and their books almost always included line engravings of picturesque street scenes, "typical" bourgeois families and obligatory views of opium smokers or dens. According to most observers, opium was a ruthless destroyer of will and ambition, turning the user into a sallow, emaciated ghost. James B. Lawrence, an American naval officer, writing of his stay in Macao in 1866, pitied those addicts "no longer able to gratify the cravings of their appetites, hanging their heads by the doors of the opium shops, which the hard-hearted keepers, having fleeced them of their all, will not permit them to enter."[40]

Hong Kong

Hong Kong (from *heang-keang,* fragrant waters) was one of the many spoils of the first Opium War, but not all British subjects considered it an asset. Henry Charles Sirr, writing in 1849, had nothing good to say about the place. The section of his book entitled "Insalubrity and Worthlessness" disparaged Hong Kong's lack of cultivable land, its pestilential summers, freezing winters, diseases such as Hong Kong fever, the vermin and the immorality of the inhabitants. In all, Sirr considered that Hong Kong, "which has been held in ill repute by the Chinese nation from time immemorial, as one of the most unhealthy, and from being the resort of pirates, thieves, and depraved characters of every description,"[41] was an out-and-out liability. Sirr's descriptions of the depravity of the opium habit rival the best of them, but his bitterness against the British for condoning the trade is really impassioned:

> The horrors and evils of this traffic are such, as to render it unbecoming Great Britain, as a Christian nation, to sanction, encourage, or permit its continuance . . . To furnish poison to the multitude, be the gain what it may, is a crime against humanity, which cries aloud to those in power to prohibit, and arrest the destroyer.[42]

Facing page: Street in the native quarter of Hong Kong, c. 1910.

This page: View of Hong Kong harbour. Woodcut, based on a photograph by Scottish photographer John Thomson, from the 1877 Hachette edition of Thomson's *Dix ans de voyage dans la Chine et l'Indo-Chine (Illustrations of China and Its People).*

Some crusaders took the opium issue personally. Edwin Joshua Dukes, an English missionary who visited China in the 1880s and who found the opium habit "destructive and immoral," wrote that "the defenders of the opium trade (who, by the way, are almost all haters of Christian missionaries) declare that our protest is an unjustifiable 'fad.' "[43]

China, of all the Asian countries, was hardest hit by the evils of opium smoking. With the focus of drug traffic moving from Canton to Shanghai, that city became a magnet for cosmopolitan travellers, down-on-their-luck refugees and criminals keen to make an easy dollar. But Thailand (Siam), Burma, Singapore, Malaysia, Borneo (Sarawak) and Vietnam (Indochina) also found themselves caught up in the conflict between condemning the vice and the need for tax revenue from opium. As colonies—except Siam, which was a protectorate of Britain and France—these countries were also subject to the greed and indifference of their colonizing parents.

The West discovered, as well, that opium smoking could not be contained in distant colonies; it spread to Europe and North America, adding yet another facet to the world's growing drug problems.

Colonialism provided an opportunity for large numbers of Europeans to live outside their own borders and to adopt and adapt fresh manners and customs. With the French settling in North Africa, Southeast Asia and the Middle East, the English in India, Egypt, East Africa and

Drug Traffic in Shanghai

Police reports on the drug trade appeared regularly in the *North China Herald*. In a case reported in 1912, police arrested a 28-year-old Latvian named Fritz Lapin for fraud. He disguised containers of flour as morphine and sold them to unsuspecting drug buyers. In a second case, police raided premises on Yunnan Road, seizing a large amount of opium along with record books that indicated the opium was disguised as "foreign medicine."[44]

"Foochow Road, Shanghai," c. 1920. Claude Farrère wrote in his story "Foochow Road" ("Fou-Tchéou-Road"): "Night having come, the entire street lights up and glows red. Each door leads to a dive, more or less bizarre, more or less alluring, but abundant with opium."[45] The sender of this postcard wrote that Shanghai was "quite thrilling."

Asia, and the Germans, Belgians, Dutch, Portuguese, Italians and Spanish in their respective colonies, Europe was awash with new ideas. Artisans were hired to redecorate the salons of fashionable society in the latest eastern styles: Chinese, Japanese, Moorish, Indian, Persian, Egyptian; handy catalogues of easily appropriated designs proliferated.

Travellers brought back tales of unparalleled danger and scandalous sensuality, along with reports of the wealth, grandeur and different mores that were at once at odds with European ways, yet were attractive because of the strangeness. For those caught in the bleakness of the Industrial Revolution, decadence had never been so appealing. What is now seen by some as a rather suspect Orientalism was then a breath of fresh air. So when opium smoking was introduced to nineteenth-century Europe by travellers returning from Asia and the Middle East, the habit flourished thanks to a growing passion for the intriguing ways of the inhabitants of these foreign lands.

INTOXICATING FUMES

"Me, I'd be there, immobile, silent, under a magnificent canopy, . . . a huge tame lion under my elbow, the naked breast of a young slave girl under my feet like a footstool, and I'd be smoking opium in a massive jade pipe."

—Théophile Gautier, *Mademoiselle de Maupin*[1]

Opium demands much from its admirers; it has to be coaxed and coddled, because, like a lover, it responds best to skilled hands. Moreover, the habitué can't simply smoke with just a pipe and a supply of opium, but has to have a "layout," a den and like-minded companions to enjoy the drug's intoxicating fumes.

The ritual becomes a precious pastime, the pipes elicit an almost mystical tenderness, and the den takes on the aura of another world. Claude Farrère wrote of an old pipe that "mysteriously evokes all of Asia" and of a "lovely *fumerie* [den] . . . with a really elegant door for leaving life and entering into the dream of the gods!"[2] Writers, in fiction, poetry and biography, have gone to great lengths to describe their experiences of opium. The poet Maurice Magre wrote, "L'esprit des Bouddhas morts habite en mon cerveau,"★ and the surrealist writer Robert Desnos claimed that "Opium, like the air, bathes those who breathe it." Rudyard Kipling simply stated: "I've seen some things that people would call strange enough; but nothing is strange when you're on the Black Smoke, except the Black Smoke."[3]

Théophile Gautier, as recorded in his essay "The Opium Pipe," went from prosaically turning in his bed like a "grilled carp" to withstanding "veils of fire and torrents of magnetic effluvia . . . inextricably and growing ever closer until sparkling wires penetrated my every pore, growing into my skin like the hair-roots in my scalp."[4]

Jean Cocteau wrote that opium "stirs up the past and the future, making them a present whole."[5]

The layout, or kit for opium smoking, consists of a pipe, a spirit lamp, a large needle and a container of opium paste, all set out on a tray. Other useful items include a scraper for cleaning out the pipe bowl, a sponge, scissors for trimming the wick of the lamp, a set of scales for measuring out the opium and extra bowls for the pipe in case of breakage. Also nice to have, though by no means necessary, are a tea service and a tobacco pipe. And for smokers too far gone or too novice to prepare their own pipes, a "chef," to "cook" the opium and keep the pipes steadily available, is a great help.

★ The spirit of dead Buddhas inhabits my brain.

Inspiration and Energy

An anonymous Newspaper Man, No. 6606, was driven to opium by fatigue. He wrote of his experiences from a jail cell, declaring that under opium's power "my brain-fag slipped from me like a discarded garment."[6]

Previous page: La Vice d'Asie: L'Opium (The Vice of Asia: Opium). This painting by Henri Vollet, exhibited at the 1909 Paris Salon, depicts an idealized Parisian opium den.

Facing page: L'Attirail d'un fumeur d'opium (A Smoker's Layout). The property of a rich Indochinese smoker: the top photo shows an elaborate pipe; the second, tea-making apparatus and a water pipe; and the third, two pipes, a lamp and a needle. From an unidentified French magazine, c. 1906. Photos by Cl. Gaudict.

Pipes

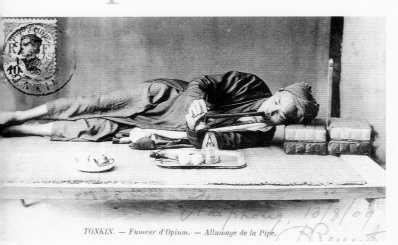

TONKIN. — *Fumeur d'Opium.* — *Allumage de la Pipe.*

Left: Fumeur d'opium (Opium Smoker). This postcard from Tonkin shows a smoker with a complete layout. R. Dufresne, Haiphong, 1909.

Below: Nineteenth-century Chinese opium pipes. The bowl of the first pipe is of redwood and is adorned with brass and copper; the metal stem is encased in eight nut shells, each carved to represent a face. The second, a beautiful example of a typical opium pipe, has a stem made of stained bamboo, decorated with finely worked white metal. The bowl rests on a white metal mount set with coloured stones.

Boxes

These two nineteenth-century ivory or bone boxes were designed to hold small, personal supplies of the gummy chandu, or smoking opium. Such opium boxes were often made of organic materials, brass, silver, cloisonné enamel, jade and a copper alloy known as *paktong*.

Scales

Nineteenth-century or early twentieth-century Chinese opium scale. This device was used to measure out small quantities of opium as well as herbs and medicines. The portable equipment consisted of a weight, a rod of ivory or bone and a small metal bowl in which the opium was placed.

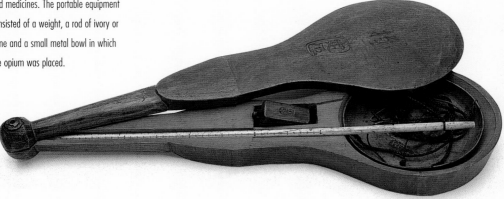

Other Pipes

Top: This tobacco pipe *(Shuey-kun)* was often erroneously used in illustrations of opium smokers. Opium could be mixed with tobacco, but this pipe was usually used for plain, finely cut tobacco.

This page, bottom: "Hitting the Pipe." The man is actually smoking a bamboo water pipe *(Shuey-yen-tong)* used for tobacco. Postcard by Charles Weidner, San Francisco, pre—1906.

Facing page, left: Another type of water pipe *(Shuey-yen-tai)* for tobacco smoking has often been mistaken for an opium pipe, as in the film *Broken Blossoms* (facing page, bottom right). This particular pipe, adorned with cloisonné enamel, is of a standard design.

Facing page, top right: "Curious Tobacco Pipes." Louis J. Beck took pains to distinguish between opium and tobacco pipes in his book *New York's Chinatown*, pp. 178—79.

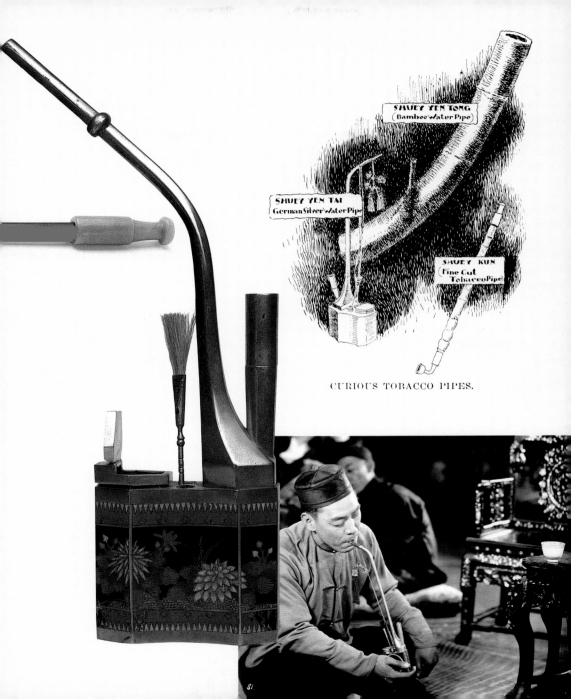

SHUEY YEN TONG
(Bamboo Water Pipe)

SHUEY YEN TAI
German Silver Water Pipe

SHUEY KUN
Fine Cut
Tobacco Pipe

CURIOUS TOBACCO PIPES.

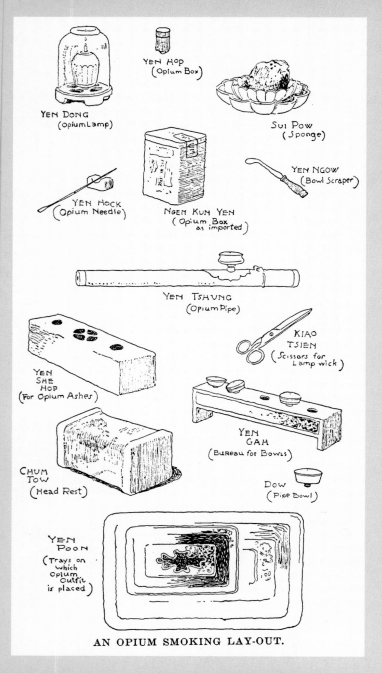

YEN DONG
(Opium Lamp)

YEN HOP
(Opium Box)

SUI POW
(Sponge)

YEN HOCK
(Opium Needle)

NGEN KUN YEN
(Opium Box as imported)

YEN NGOW
(Bowl Scraper)

YEN TSHUNG
(Opium Pipe)

YEN SHE HOP
(For Opium Ashes)

KIAO TSIEN
(Scissors for Lamp wick)

CHUM TOW
(Head Rest)

YEN GAH
(Bureau for Bowls)

DOW
(Pipe Bowl)

YEN POON
(Trays on which Opium Outfit is placed)

AN OPIUM SMOKING LAY-OUT.

This page: An elaborate layout, with almost everything the opium smoker would need. Working down from the top: spirit lamp, personal opium box, sponge, needle, commercial opium box, bowl scraper, pipe, container for ashes, scissors, head rest, stand for bowls, spare bowl and tray. From Louis J. Beck's *New York's Chinatown*, 1898, p. 148.

Facing page: The wealthy Chinese opium smoker, seated, has before him a spirit lamp, a bowl scraper, needles, a set of scales with the weight and dish laid out on the table, and a stand with extra bowls. A lovely wood engraving, but inaccurate, as opium smoking was difficult to manage while seated thus. From an unidentified French journal, c. 1889. Credited to Georges Massias and Dietrich.

"Suddenly, magically, a bamboo shot up, then a poppy, then a flame. The Stranger broke the stem of the bamboo and plucked the poppy. As if by a spell, the bamboo became adorned with gold and jade, and the knot blossomed into a bowl. The poppy heads oozed a liquor like black honey. This was the first pipe and the first opium."

—Claude Farrère, "La Sagesse de l'Empereur"[7]

★ Yen

Those who claim they have a "yen," or a desire, for something, are using a word directly related to opium. *Yen* or *yen-yen* means a craving for opium.

The opium pipe may well have grown out of the legend related by Claude Farrère in *Fumée d'opium,* so unusual and so specific is it to the art and ritual of opium smoking. A love affair with a pipe is due, in part, to the pipe's extraordinary usefulness in bringing the smoker pleasure. In return, the smoker faithfully tends it, taking care to clean out the ash—the *yen shee,* ★ as it was known in Chinese dens—so that it draws well.

Distinctive in shape, the typical opium pipe consists of an 18- to 24-inch-long hollow shaft of bamboo or ebony, sealed at one end and with a mouthpiece at the other. About three quarters of the way down the shaft from the mouthpiece, there is a removable hollow bowl, or damper, of metal, porcelain or clay, pierced at the top with a small hole in which the opium is

placed. A metal collar encircles the pipe and secures the bowl tightly, ensuring that the smoke can escape only through the mouthpiece.

The style of the pipe often reflects the wealth or poverty of the owner. Stems of elaborate pipes may be made of amber or rare ivory, or ornamented with tortoise-shell or filigreed metal and semi-precious jewels. Others may be decorated with cloisonné enamels and adorned with inscriptions and patterns. The mouthpiece and corresponding tip at the other end may be of jade, jadeite or ivory. Basic pipes are completely unadorned and of the simplest bamboo and clay. Bamboo pipes are preferred by the serious smoker; they absorb the drug, becoming "sweetened" over time.[8]

Une fumerie d'opium en Chine (An Opium Den in China). The original caption reads: "Rich people have everything in their houses, including a room where they can close themselves up and surrender to their degrading and fatal vice." The woman and the boy soothe the smoker with music while he prepares his own pipes. From an article entitled "Pavots d'Asie: Fleurs de Morts des Races Jaunes" ("The Poppies of Asia: The Yellow Race's Flowers of Death") in *Lectures pour tous,* 1899, p. 500.

Pipe and poppy decoration from A. P. Quirmbach's *From Opium Fiend to Preacher*, 1907.

The Sanctity of Opium

Although smokers probably had strict rules and taboos attached to smoking opium, some of those, as reported by Western observers, seem rather suspect. H. H. Kane noted that in China, women were not permitted to smoke a beloved bamboo pipe, lest the moisture from their saliva cause the stem to split. Mordecai C. Cooke, the author of *The Seven Sisters of Sleep,* believed that opium smokers inhaled so deeply that every membrane was saturated, thus causing the smoke to be exhaled not only through nose and mouth but also through ears and eyes.[10]

The Shanghai Gesture

POPPY: He didn't bring the pipe, the—damned jackass!
OSHIMA: Let us not have—the pipe, Poppy—it is—no good!
POPPY [Screaming.]: I want a pipe—I tell you!
　　[Stamps her foot.] I will have a pipe![9]

In John Colton's brutal play *The Shanghai Gesture* (1926), Poppy, the daughter of Sir Guy Charteris, the Taipan, or big boss, of the British China Trading Co., has been lured into a life of dissipation—drinking, smoking opium and probably things much worse—by "Mother God Damn," who is using the young woman to get back at Sir Guy for spurning her many years before. In the 1941 movie of the same name, Mother God Damn's name has been tempered to "Mother Gin Sling," and the only reference that remains to opium is an obscure one—the girl's nickname, Poppy.

L. Crespin, Saigon

75. - Préparation d'une Pipe d'opium

This page and facing page: Préparation d'une Pipe d'opium (Preparation of an Opium Pipe) *and Fumeur d'opium sur le lit de camp* (Opium Smoker on His Camp Cot). It is not unusual to find postcards shot in the same room with the same paraphernalia and smoker(s) but in a variety of poses. L. Crespin, Saigon, c. 1926.

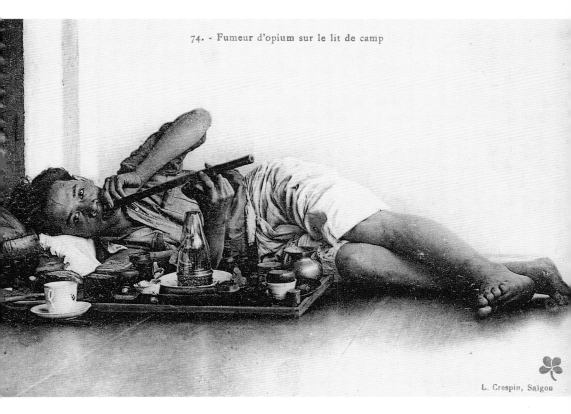

74. - Fumeur d'opium sur le lit de camp

L. Crespin, Saïgon

"Opium teaches only one thing, which is that aside from physical suffering, there is nothing real."—André Malraux, *Man's Fate*[11]

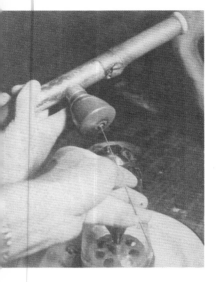

The opium smoker, whether in a den in the south of France, in a room off an alley in San Francisco or in the home of a rich Mandarin in Canton, follows a well-established procedure.

The layout is assembled, the spirit lamp is lit, and the smoker makes himself comfortable, as opium is most efficiently smoked in the reclining position. Taking a pea-size ball, or pill, of the dark brown opium paste, or chandu, with the end of a long blunt needle, he holds it over the flame of the lamp until the opium bubbles and swells and turns golden. In some accounts the smoker lets the ball catch fire, blows the

flame out, and catches the opium on the edge of the pipe bowl, stretching the gooey mass into long strings in order to "cook" it better, repeating the process several times until it is deemed properly cooked, at which point he rolls it back into its pea shape and quickly pushes it into the hole in the bowl.[12] Holding the bowl of the pipe close to the lamp so that the flame hits the

A Glossary for the Den

The den:
joint
hop joint
lay-down joint
The pipe:
gonger
bamboo
dream stick
saxophone
The smoker:
pipie
pipefiend
gowster
hop-head
yenshee boy
To smoke opium:
To be on the hip
Kicking the gong around★
Rolling the log

★ Movie buffs will recall the line "When he kicked old Buddha's gong" in the Hoagy Carmichael song "Hong Kong Blues" in the film *To Have and Have Not* (U.S. 1945).

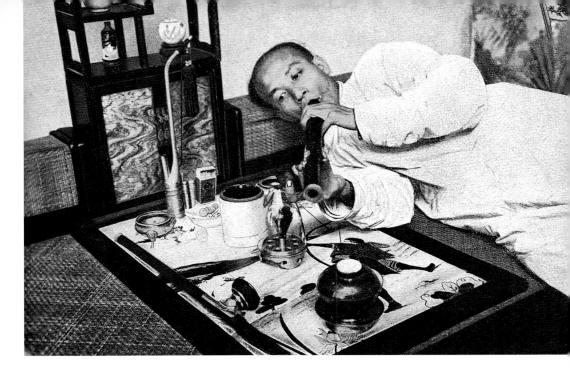

ball of opium, the smoker takes deep pulls at the pipe until
the opium is completely consumed. Depending on the depth
of the draw, this could be accom-
plished in one inhalation or several.[13]

When the pipe is cool, the smoker prepares more
opium, smokes, prepares still more, and continues until he
is satisfied. A novice smoker might consume three pipes; a
veteran needs to smoke a great many more.

An odour, considered either enticing or repulsive,
emanates from the burning drug. Edwin Joshua Dukes, a
missionary in China in the 1880s, described the smell as "vile
and sickening."[14] James B. Lawrence noted that "The fumes
are not unpleasant; in fact, they have rather an attraction."[15]

"There is always a need for intoxication: [China] has opium, Islam has hashish, the West has woman. . . . Perhaps love is above all the means which the Occidental uses to free himself from man's fate. . . ."—André Malraux, *Man's Fate*[16]

An English Opium Odalisque

In his novel *Dope,* Sax Rohmer described the effect that entering a deluxe opium den had on novice lady opium smokers: " 'The idea of undressing and reclining on these divans in real Oriental fashion,' declared Mollie, giggling, 'makes me feel that I am an odalisque already. I have dreamed that I was an odalisque, dear— after smoking, you know. It was heavenly.' " [19]

Wealthy Chinese opium smokers in a private salon. From *The Living Races of Mankind,* p. 211, c. 1900.

H. H. Kane, the author of *Opium-Smoking in America and China,* thought the cooking opium had a "pleasant creamy odor" and the smoke "a not unpleasant fruity odor." Bertha, a smoker quoted in Louis J. Beck's *New York's Chinatown,* claimed that it smelled "something like peanuts roasting." Novelist Graham Greene wrote in his diary that the smell of opium "was like the first sight of a beautiful woman with whom one realizes that a relationship is possible." [17]

If the art and artifice of opium paraphernalia contribute to the drug's mystique, the den does so on a grander scale. Descriptions of opium dens vary wildly, depending on the imagination of the writer. Graphic accounts of luxuriously elegant dens strain credibility with their handsome tapestries, comfortable cushions and mats, soft lighting, and solicitous attendants dressed in traditional costume, waiting patiently to prepare the pipes. These dreamy dens are features of fiction and rarely appear in factual accounts.

In *Dope,* a fast-paced novel by Sax Rohmer, high society Londoners frequent an atmospheric "House of a Hundred Raptures" adorned with Oriental tapestries and rugs, hidden away in a wretched abandoned building and overseen by the officiating priestess, Mrs. Sin, a voluptuous "Cuban-Jewess." In *The Yellow Claw,* another novel by Rohmer, London dens are referred to as "temples" and the attendants as "minor priests." [18]

Real opium dens were quite squalid, often nothing more than makeshift rooms that could be easily disguised or dismantled at a moment's notice. Smokers took turns lying on filthy mats strewn on unswept floors, the air was heavy with cloying smoke since the rooms were well sealed to prevent the escape of telltale fumes, and the customers were more likely to be unkempt addicts rather than rich Persian princes. And these were for westerners. The Chinese opium dens, judging from the descriptions of the day, were even more unsavoury. Reporters and crusaders took a vicious glee in emphasizing the sordidness. Louis J. Beck's description of a real den in New York in 1898 pretty much sums it up:

Beginning at a point about three feet from the floor are several separate and distinct strata of smoke which rise and fall like the bosom of the sea disturbed by a swell. The pungent odor which greets you at the door is intensified a hundredfold, and is heavy and sensuous. A score of little lamps dot the place here and there, and are burning bravely, as if they were trying to light up the surroundings. Their attempt at illumination is a failure . . . Vice loves gloom and goes hand in hand with darkness. Here is vice of the vilest kind—imported vice. On either side of the room there is a row of board bunks, as habitués say, erected about two feet from the floor and covered . . . with matting and dotted with wooden head rests or little wads of straw . . . which serve as pillows. This is the hour for the fiends, and there is little unoccupied space on the bunks.[20]

A Chinatown "joint." From *New York's Chinatown*, 1898, by Louis J. Beck, p. 157.

"Opium unites the souls of smokers who recline around the same lamp. It's a bath in a thick atmosphere, a reunion in one bed with heavy covers, a veritable coupling that one can't resist. It's perhaps because of this that there are so few solitary smokers, why, in spite of themselves, they advertise their poison. There is, certainly, in each opium addict, an unhappy or unsatisfied lover."—Robert Desnos, *Le Vin est tiré . . .*[21]

Socializing in opium dens was very important, not for the conversation, which was essentially nonexistent, but for the mere presence of other bodies. Rare were the smokers—in literature or factual accounts—who chose to smoke alone.

Jean Cocteau, writer, artist, opium smoker and author of *Opium: The Diary of a Cure,* personally disliked company. He wrote: "Smoking *à deux* is already crowded. Smoking *à trois* is difficult. Smoking *à quatre* is impossible."[22]

The intimacy of the den struck writer Louis Latzarus, a contributor to *Voilà,* a French weekly scandal sheet, as beneath contempt:

One day I went into one of these sanctuaries, and I looked with curiosity at the men and women draped in kimonos who, without disgust, passed a pipe from one to one another, putting it to their lips, even though they would have shivered with horror at the idea of sharing the same spoon. Their solemn faces made me want to laugh . . . I contemplated them, while smoking an honest French cigarette, and when I'd seen enough I got up to go.[23]

"During my lifetime, I had smoked my weight in opium, and even more since my ego died. And opium was the cause of that."—Claude Farrère, "Le Palais Rouge"[24]

Fumée d'opium

Claude Farrère's principal work, the infamous *Fumée d'opium (Black Opium),* first published in its entirety in 1904, was a series of short stories linked thematically by opium. Drawing

on his observations and experiences in the French navy, Claude Farrère, born Frédéric-Charles Bargone (1867–1957), wove his stories as sinuously as smoke curls from a pipe; they are dreamy, hallucinatory escapes. With Farrère, the reader visits dens in China, Saigon, Paris and Toulon. He, more than any other author, intoxicates with the abstraction of the act of smoking, the atmosphere, the fumes. Reading Farrère is more than just a vicarious smoke.

The lurid, "shocking" cover on the 1958 Berkley reprint of *Black Opium,* with its vision of a naked woman, implies a connection between opium smoking and sexual ecstasy. Nothing could be further from the truth: for men, that is. Over and over, as Farrère describes the effects of smoking ten, twenty, sixty pipes of opium at one session, it is obvious that smokers are in no condition to blink their eyelids let alone fulfill such fantasies. His dens are filled with indolent, pleasure-seeking men and women, all stretched out languorously, focussed only on savouring their pipes.

Did He or Didn't He?

Did Farrère smoke opium? He is quoted as saying that he didn't, but his vivid descriptions beg the question. His intimate knowledge of opium, his stay in Turkey and voyages to the East, his opium-smoking literary circle—Edmond Jaloux and Paul-Jean Toulet among many—and his pro-opium pamphlet, "L'opium ou l'alcool" in 1920, all weigh the odds in favour of his use of opium.[25]

Left: Claude Farrère. Undated photograph credited to G. L. Manuel Frères.

Facing page: Black Opium. Cover of the Berkley Books 1958 reprint of the English translation of Claude Farrère's *Fumée d'opium.*

BERKLEY
BOOKS

G-120

35¢

BLACK OPIUM

**Claude
Farrère**

Women figure strongly in the world of opium, as embodiments of forsaken convention and the breakdown of traditional society, and as symbols of decadence. Female habituées found dens more liberating and welcoming than bars. The reputation of dens as hotbeds of passionate abandon no doubt came from the freedom with which women were able to conduct themselves and from the simple fact that they stretched out in mixed company and gave themselves up to a somnolent narcotic.

Caucasian women, as opium smokers, opium den proprietors, or as wives or concubines of Asian opium dealers, added a sensual overtone to the smoking ritual and so were a favourite topic amongst writers who frequented or imagined opium dens. But their presence, especially in strait-laced North America, was a slap in the face to society's strict boundaries.

The American and Canadian anti-opium crusaders Willard B. Farwell and Judge Emily Murphy both wrote about women smokers as victims. Murphy, despondent about the endless stream of young girls appearing in her court, wrote: "You may attempt something in the way of salvage, only to find that to reform [them] would be about as difficult as making Eve from the original rib."[26]

Few women, however, have written about their motivation for smoking opium. Unlike laudanum, and to a lesser extent morphine, which have their share of noteworthy female chroniclers, women's stories and accounts of smoking have been relegated to obscurity.

Women Write About Opium Smoking:

Santa Louise Anderson, "An Opium Dream," 1879; Pearl Buck, *Dragon Seed,* 1941, *Pavilion of Women,* 1946; Colette, *Le Pur et l'impur,* 1932; Caresse Crosby, *The Passionate Years,* 1979; Emily Hahn, "The Big Smoke" (n.d.); Maud Diver, *The Great Amulet,* 1913; Mary "Perdita" Robinson, "The Maniac" (n.d.); Grace Thompson Seton, *Poison Arrows: Strange Journey with an Opium Dreamer,* 1938; May Churchill Sharpe, *Chicago May: Her Story: Goings on in Limehouse* (n.d.).

Pages 76–77: A series of American stereocards showing the seduction of white women by "Chinese" opium smokers. These were sold to titillate rather than to enrage. c. 1910.

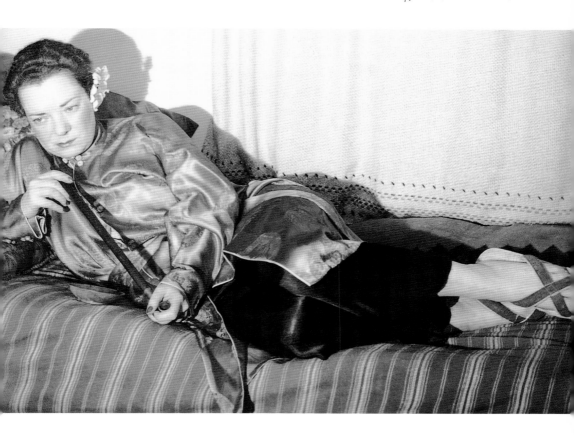

This Caucasian woman, dressed in "Oriental" finery and posing as an opium smoker is, in fact, holding a tobacco pipe. Her layout consists of a saucer in which to dump the ashes.

"As most of the female smokers are prostitutes, and as attempts at self-destruction are not uncommon amongst this class, this is not surprising and need not be laid at the door of opium." —H. H. Kane, *Opium-Smoking in America and China*[27]

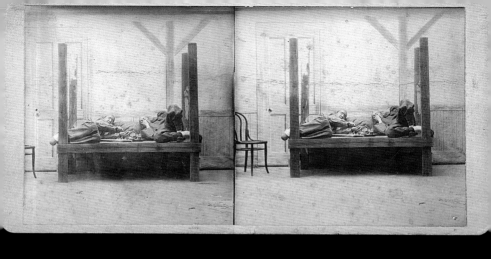

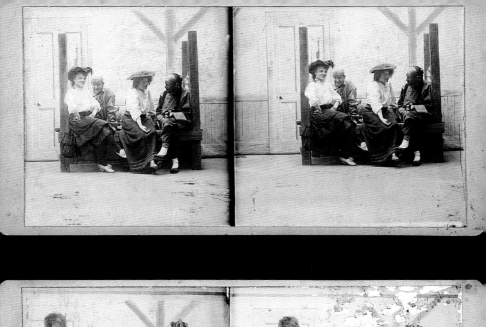

SHANGHI   GAL

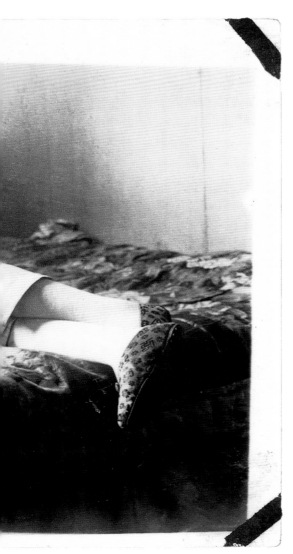

"I had always wanted to be an opium addict."—Emily Hahn, "The Big Smoke"[28]

Emily Hahn

The 1920s and '30s were extraordinary decades for independent young women. This period between the First and Second World Wars was a time of unprecedented freedom, and the budding writer Emily Hahn (1901–97) took advantage of this, travelling to Africa in 1930 and then to Asia in 1935, after graduating as the University of Wisconsin's first female mining engineer.[29] Hahn stayed on in China during the Second World War and wrote a number of articles, many for *The New Yorker*, including two on her drug experiences, "The Big Smoke" and "Bhang."

"Shanghi Gal." This view of a solitary woman smoker and her surroundings captures the essence of opium's languid appeal. Uncredited photograph, c. 1920.

Other ways to smoke

In Egypt and Turkey, opium was smoked in a considerably different manner. According to Edward W. Lane, author of *The Manners and Customs of the Modern Egyptians* (1836), Egyptians smoked opium combined with hashish, a mixture known as *maagoon* or *barsh*.[30]

When opium was smoked in Turkey and the Levant, it was mixed with tobacco and placed in a tobacco pipe or the water pipe known as a *narguileh*. Those who "ate" opium either drank it or took it in the form of small pills, both often flavoured to disguise the bitter taste.

In India, opium was both smoked and eaten, particularly amongst the poor in the state of Assam, and in such huge quantities that it provoked public concern. Raw opium was decocted into a paste, mixed with fried betel leaves and then smoked in a bamboo pipe called a *hookah*. Opium eating was far more common than smoking, probably because of the amount of preparation required of smoking.[31]

Café Turc (Turkish Café). The men are smoking narguilehs—water pipes with the mouthpiece at the end of a long flexible tube. Although tobacco was the smoke of choice at such cafés, opium would occasionally be added. Postcard from a photograph by E. F. Rochat, Constantinople, c. 1900.

Right: Photograph taken in an unidentified village in India. The woman seated, centre, is smoking a hookah, a bamboo pipe often used in India for smoking opium or opium mixed with fried betel leaves. Undated.

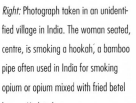

Left: "Hashish Coffee House." This postcard shows a posed scene at a typical Egyptian coffee house. The man on the far left is holding a *gôzeh,* a modified narguileh used for smoking hashish. According to E. W. Lane, author of *The Manners and Customs of the Modern Egyptians,* this "pernicious" habit was adopted mainly by the lower classes.[32] Produced in France, c. 1910, for a booklet of tear-out cards entitled *Egyptian Types and Scenes.*

Le Petit Parisien

SUPPLÉMENT LITTÉRAIRE ILLUSTRÉ

TOUS LES JOURS
Le Petit Parisien
(Six pages)
5 centimes

CHAQUE SEMAINE
LE SUPPLÉMENT LITTÉRAIRE
5 centimes

DIRECTION: 18, rue d'Enghien (10e). PARIS

ABONNEMENTS

PARIS ET DÉPARTEMENTS :
12 mois, 4 fr.50. 6 mois, 2 fr.25
UNION POSTALE :
12 mois, 5 fr. 50. 6 mois, 3 fr.

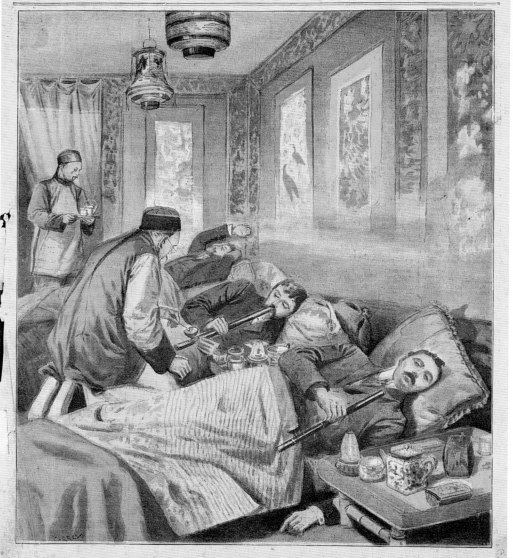

UNE FUMERIE D'OPIUM EN FRANCE

THE WRITER'S MUSE

" VIE : RÊVE
OPIUM : RÉALITÉ " ★

—Claude Farrère, *Fumée d'opium* [1]

Une fumerie d'opium en France (An Opium Den in France). The accompanying brief article deplores the spread of opium use in France (particularly in the Mediterranean port of Toulon), noting that "there are already more than enough alcoholics and absinthe drinkers to destroy the vigour of the people. Let's not add to this numberless army the sad flock of opium smokers." Cover illustration (signed Carrey) from *Le Petit Parisien,* 17 February 1907.

★ LIFE: DREAM
OPIUM: REALITY

The European fascination with life in the East and the drugs easily available there was mirrored and popularized on the written page. Travellers to Turkey published numerous tales of hashish and opium eating. Baron Alphonse du Tott, who visited Constantinople in the 1780s, observed the Turkish opium eaters who frequented the drug market, noting that "their pale and melancholy figures would be sufficient to raise our pity, did not their lengthened necks, their heads turned on one side, their back bone distorted, their shoulders raised up to their ear, and a number of other extravagant attitudes, which result from their disease, exhibit a picture of the most ridiculous kind." [2]

French translator, poet and playwright Gérard de Nerval (1808–55) visited Egypt, Lebanon and Turkey in 1843, resulting in his book *Voyage en Orient,* largely composed of quasi-imaginary tales. One of them, entitled

CHATEAUBRIAND.

"Hashish," tells of a weary Moslem traveller who, offered hashish, at first refuses, saying that it is forbidden. When told that "every source of pleasure is always forbidden," he relents, tastes it, then declares that "Hashish renders you equal to God."[3]

In 1857, the writer Théophile Gautier (1811–72) published his book *Constantinople*, an account of his travels from Malta to Turkey. He frequented Istanbul's Scutari Cemetery, savouring its "romantic charm" and the opportunities it afforded him to smoke his pipe sitting on a tomb, "an action that would seem irreverent [in Paris]." Gautier, who had experimented with hashish and opium in Paris in the 1840s, also wrote: "I give myself up to the sweetness of the *kif,* a little benumbed by fatigue and the opium-laced tobacco that I've put in my pipe."[4]

Gautier was heavily influenced by his experiments with hashish and opium. His fanciful short story "La Pipe d'opium," written in 1838, was followed by two others called "Haschisch" and "Le Club des Haschichins."

Although a vice with a long heritage in Asia, in Europe opium smoking was an afterthought, following on the heels of and competing with laudanum and morphine.

In France, the craving for the exotic that manifested itself in architecture, literature and art created a state of mind ripe for drug experimentation.

Chateaubriand

French writer François-René de Chateaubriand (1768–1848) wrote of his travels in the Middle East in 1806:

"It was midnight when we arrived at the khan of Menemen ... Sitting on the carpets, their legs crossed, were the Turkish merchants grouped around the fire over which slaves prepared the pilaf; other travellers smoked their pipes at the door of the khan, ate opium and listened to stories."[5]

US LES
MANCHES

DU PETIT JOURNAL
ET SON SUPPLÉMENT AGRICOLE
GRAND HEBDOMADAIRE POUR TOUS

50 C.

22-10-33

UNE FUMERIE D'OPIUM SUR UNE TOMBE

...i Effendi, riche marchand d'opium de Stamboul, étant décédé subitement, ses amis, pour honorer
...mémoire, s'assemblèrent au cimetière d'Eyoub, où il était inhumé et organisèrent une fumerie
sur son tombeau.

Théophile Gautier and Gérard de Nerval brought their fascination with opium and the ways of the East back to France as did Maxime Du Camp, writer, photographer and travelling companion of the writer Gustave Flaubert. Du Camp's novel *Mémoires d'un suicidé,* about an opium eater who commits suicide, was inspired by a trip to the Middle East during the years 1849–51.

Around 1845, a number of writers formed the Club des Haschichins with the goal of experimenting with hashish and opium. Held at the Île Saint-Louis apartments of the painter Fernand Boissard de Boisdenier, frequenters included writers Nerval and Gautier, along with Honoré de Balzac, Charles Baudelaire and Alphonse Karr, and the artists Eugène Delacroix and Honoré Daumier.[6]

Jules Verne (1828–1905) tried his hand at "oriental" fiction with his short story "The Tribulations of a Chinaman in China," about Kin-Fo, a Chinese merchant in Shanghai who considers suicide by overdosing on opium smoking. In his *Around the World in Eighty Days,* the success of Phileas Fogg's attempts to win a wager by encircling the globe are jeopardized when Fogg's assistant, the Frenchman Passepartout,

Page 84: Engraving of François-René de Chateaubriand. His *Itinéraire de Paris à Jérusalem* (1811) influenced a number of writers of the time. From *Ridpath's History of the World,* 1899, p. 464.

Page 85: Une fumerie d'opium sur une tombe (A Tombside Opium Den). The caption for this cover of the 22 October 1933 *L'Illustré* reads: "The memory of Zeki Effendi, a rich Istanbul opium merchant . . . is honoured by his friends. They met at the Eyoub Cemetery— where he is buried—and organized an opium smoking ceremony on his tomb."

This page: Théophile Gautier. From *Théophile Gautier* by Maxime Du Camp, 1907, frontispiece. Uncredited photograph taken in 1866.

À la morphine

Jules Verne wrote the poem "À la morphine" (1886) after taking the drug to relieve the pain from a bullet wound in his leg inflicted by his nephew, Gaston.[7]

collapses in Hong Kong under the effects of smoking an opium pipe given to him by an enemy.

Jean Lorrain (1855–1906) travelled to North Africa and wrote prolifically during his relatively short and troubled life. His novel *Monsieur de Phocas* (1901) is the story of a man whose morbid state of mind drives him to seek relief. Acquaintances are convinced that his "eyes are surely the eyes of a smoker of opium. He carries the drunken burden of hemp in his veins. Opium is like syphilis . . . it is a thing which stays for years and years in the blood."[8] Although set in Paris, the book is infused with Oriental sensuality.

The exuberant French writer Guillaume Apollinaire (1880–1918) smoked opium occasionally when in Montmartre around 1910, and quite intensely when in Nice in 1914. At this time he was besotted with Louise de Coligny-Châtillon, otherwise known as Lou, who loved him well enough, but only inside the opium den; outside of it, she appeared to have an aversion towards him. Apollinaire, who wrote Lou packets of passionate and tortured love letters, was aware of her feelings: "He knew, that for her, he only existed when they smoked."[9]

"La Mandoline l'œillet et le bambou" ("The Mandolin Carnation and the Bamboo"), a *calligramme*, by Guillaume Apollinaire, c. 1914.

LA MANDOLINE L'ŒILLET ET LE BAMBOU

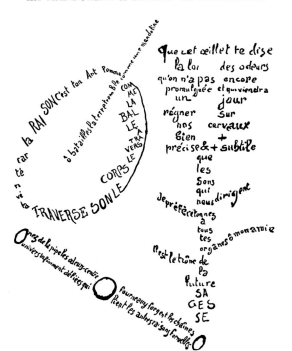

Charles Baudelaire

Charles Baudelaire (1821–67), the author of *Les Fleurs du Mal* (1857), a collection of poems, played a significant role in the awareness of drugs in nineteenth-century France. He translated De Quincey's *Confessions* and the works of Edgar Allan Poe into French, and wrote essays on opium and hashish for the *Revue contemporaine*. These were later published as *Les Paradis artificiels* (1851), a book which has often been compared to *Confessions*, although "On Wine and Hashish" and "Hashish" do not discuss opium, and much of "An Opium Eater" is simply a reflection on De Quincey's work.

An imaginative, flamboyant man, Baudelaire was an occasional visitor to the Club des Haschichins, but he was not an opium smoker; rather, he became addicted to laudanum.

"Et les moins sots, hardis amants de la Démence,

Fuyant le grand troupeau parqué par le Destin,

Et se réfugiant dans l'opium immense!"★

—Baudelaire, "Le Voyage"[10]

Sed non Satia

"More than fidelity, opium,
  night,

I desire the elixir of your
    lips where love flaunts
    itself."

—from *Les Fleurs du Mal*[14]

Among the poems in *Les Fleurs du Mal* that contain references to opium are "Le Voyage," dedicated to Maxime Du Camp, and "Le Poison," which proclaims, "Opium can expand space without boundaries / stretch the limitless."[11]

With critical success slow in coming, Baudelaire lived a hand-to-mouth existence, often borrowing money from his mother or other relatives to support his extravagant ways. Venereal disease took a heavy toll on his health, leaving him debilitated and, towards the end of his life, semi-paralysed. Although opium was not prescribed for syphilis, it was recommended as a counter to the cathartic effect that mercury—which was prescribed—had on the bowels. According to biographer Claude Pichois, Baudelaire resorted to laudanum on a daily basis. He likened opium to a woman friend, "an old and terrible friend, and, alas! like them all, full of caresses and deceptions."[12]

From 1862 on, Baudelaire's health declined rapidly. Often gripped by colds, headaches, fever and rheumatism, he was a walking medicine chest, taking pills that contained opium, valerian, digitalis and quinine, and doubling the dose because of his habituation to the opium.[13] Baudelaire died in September 1867.

★ And the least foolish, intrepid lovers of disorder,
  Fleeing the herd restrained by Destiny,
  Take refuge in Opium's vastness!

Among those in Apollinaire's Montmartre circle was Pablo Picasso, who said, so Jean Cocteau claimed, that "The smell of opium is the least stupid smell in the world." Another artist, Francis Picabia, wrote in his thinly disguised autobiographical novel, *Caravansérail* (1924), of smoking in the hôtel des Séraphins, where "the second floor was rigorously reserved for smokers, thus giving the inhabitants on the first and third floors a delicious calm."[15]

> *"Boy, une pipe encore. Douce m'en soit l'aubaine*
> *Et l'or aérien où s'étouffent les pas*
> *Du Sommeil. Main non, reste, ô boy: n'entends-tu pas*
> *Le dieu muet qui heurte à la porte d'ébène?"*★
> —Paul-Jean Toulet, *Les Contrerimes*[16]

★ Boy, another pipe. Sweet to me be this chance And the airborne gold where sleep's steps are muffled. But no, stay, o boy, don't you hear The silent god who knocks at the ebony door?

The poet Paul-Jean Toulet (1867–1920) is notorious for his collection of opium-hazed poems called *Les Contrerimes*. Toulet had travelled extensively, visiting Algeria, Spain, Singapore and Indochina, and was a seeker of pleasure; he drank continuously and experimented with opium and ether. Once having tried hashish, he declared: "Now I know what death is!" He favoured opium, however, becoming an acknowledged connoisseur, so it was to him that Colette's husband, Willy (Henri Gauthier-Villars), turned for his expertise when writing his novel *Lélie, fumeuse d'opium* (1911).[17]

Facing page, left: Alfred Jarry. An uncredited, undated photograph published in *Alfred Jarry ou la Naissance, la Vie et la Mort du Père Ubu (Alfred Jarry, or the Birth, Life and Death of Père Ubu)*, 1932.

Facing page, right: Portrait of André Salmon by Pablo Picasso, 1904.
© *Pablo Picasso 1998 \ VIS*ART Copyright Inc.*

Maurice Magre (1877–1942), another writer influenced by opium, wrote *Les Soirs d'opium,* a collection of seductively amoral and sensual poems that is a testimony to his absolute intoxication with the drug.

André Salmon (1881–1969), writer, art critic and possibly France's most prolific name dropper, tried out some Benares opium with writer and regular opium smoker René Dalize at a *ravissante* bachelor-pad *fumerie* near Paris's chic parc Monceau. He complained that, even though the den was far from being low class, the rich patron annoyed them to no end. Dalize, a marine officer and writer, had little money but was able to afford to smoke regularly, because, as Salmon observed, "Before 1914 smoking cost less than going to a café." Salmon also smoked opium with Paul-Jean Toulet, who, according to Salmon, smoked properly, in that he made no pretense at having visions, ecstasies or other idiotic literary manifestations.[18]

Alfred Jarry (1873–1907), author of *Ubu roi,* was an absinthomaine but experimented with hashish and opium as well. His "L'Opium" (1893) is a dense, nightmarish tale that opens with the narrator's astral self visiting the morgue (morgue visits were a common pastime in nineteenth-century Paris). After a series of

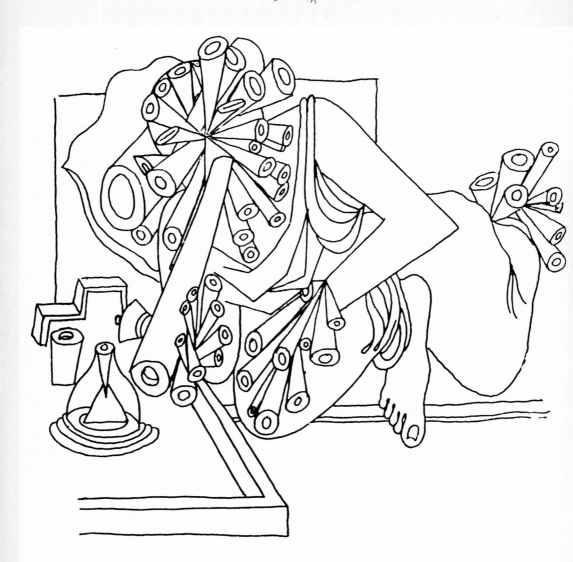

bizarre encounters, he finds himself on a train from the country of Opium, then hears bacchanalian incantations and sees an orchestra made up of cardinals and bishops accompanied by the pope keeping time. Walls fall away; vaults rise into the air like balloons; columns grow, stretching out the "Titanesque architecture." Suddenly, the narrator finds himself back in his terrestrial body, needing to refill his opium narguileh.[19]

The imagination of Jean Cocteau (1889–1963), poet, writer, filmmaker, novelist and artist, no doubt benefited from his frequent sorties into the world of opium. Cocteau, a veteran opium smoker by the time he checked in for a cure at a Saint Cloud clinic in 1928,[20] produced a work called *Opium: The Diary of a Cure.* It is a startling book, not the least because of the powerful images drawn by Cocteau during his stay.

Cocteau overstayed his welcome at the clinic, but his departing words left doubt as to the efficacy of the treatment:

The work which exploits me needed opium; it needed me to leave opium; once more, I will be taken in. And I was wondering, shall I take opium or not? . . . I will take it if my work wants me to.

And if opium wants me to.[21]

Drawing #31 by Jean Cocteau from *Opium: The Diary of a Cure* (1930). Reproduced with the kind permission of Peter Owen Ltd. and Comité Jean Cocteau.

And it did want him to. Cocteau resumed opium smoking and continued to produce astonishing work.[22]

The next wave of opium writers included Robert Desnos (1900–45), who wrote from personal familiarity with cocaine, heroin and opium.[23] His novel *Le Vin est tiré . . .* (1943), set in the thirties, about a group of young Parisian addicts, is completely occupied with drugs.

Poet Roger Gilbert-Lecomte (1907–41), founder of the revue *Le Grand Jeu*, was the author of the poem "Rêve opiace" (1924) and a story entitled "Monsieur Morphée, empoissoneur public" (1930). In his increasingly hallucinatory correspondence with friends and colleagues, he wrote of smoking "tabac opiacé" and made frequent references to opium as "le Dieu noir," "la Reine," "le Grand Tabac" and "le sang noir."[24] Gilbert-Lecomte tried a cure but in the end turned to injecting morphine as it was cheaper and more effective than opium smoking.

Colette (1873–1954), in her novel *Le Pur et l'impur* (1932), wrote about an opium den somewhere in Paris: "Quite expecting to be bored, I settled down on the mat allotted to me and watched the opium smoke wastefully and sluggishly streaming upward to collide, as if regretfully, with the glass panes of the skylight."[25]

Colette. Undated photograph, credited to Henri Manuel.

The appeal of opium smoking was not limited to literary circles. Sailors had brought back the opium-smoking habit from their stints in the Far East, and because of them numerous opium dens were established in port cities such as Brest, Nantes, Cherbourg, Toulon and Marseille. According to Arnould de Liedekerke, author of *La Belle*

Paris Dens

Some Parisian *fumeries* (the number at the end of each address refers to the quarter or *arrondisement*):

17, quai d'Anjou, Île Saint-Louis, L'hôtel de Pimodan, home to the Club des Haschichins (4th); place Blanche (9th); Ternes (17th); rue de la Huchette (5th); Saint-Ouen; (17th); blvd. Thiers (16th); rue Soufflot (5th) and rue de la Tour, the first den to be run by a Chinese host, established in 1880 by a Tsin Ling (16th).[29]

époque d'opium, Toulon, a relatively small town, had more than 200 dens by 1905.[26]

By the late nineteenth century, opium dens had sprung up all over France. According to sources cited in Jean-Jacques Yvorel's *Les Poisons de l'esprit,* contradictory reports claimed that by 1901 Paris had from 56 to more than 1200 establishments for smoking opium.[27]

Opium smoking was so prevalent in the French navy that it was the target of incensed articles such as one in *La Grimace* (1917) and figured in a number of novels, including *Les Civilisés* (1905) and *Les Petites alliées* (1908), both by Claude Farrère who was a naval officer as well as a novelist.

Farrère attempted to lobby the French government to hold an inquiry into the opium question but was unable to drum up any official support. He also decried the hypocrisy of the French, who could break the career of a naval officer suspected of smoking opium—the initials F.O., *fumeur d'opium,* beside an individual's name were fatal for his career—but who gave out licences for the sale of opium in Indochina.[28]

La Grimace

In 1917, *La Grimace,* a weekly journal devoted to satire, politics, literature and theatre, ran an article entitled "Les Empoisonneurs de l'Armée" ("The Poisoners of the Army"), one of a series giving blow-by-blow accounts of military officers who were notorious addicts, among whom were Officer Robert S., fervent drug proselytizer and son of a highly placed magistrate, and deserter Lieutenant D. of Brest. All were thieves and spies, and all were arrested while they were acting under the influence of opium. The ordinary citizen, too, was caught up in this immoral world; drug peddlers, particularly women, targeted soldiers, and smuggling to supply the market was on the increase.

The author of the article, Léo Poldés, pointed out that the drug problem was exacerbated by the availability of morphine and cocaine. These were drugs, he claimed, of German manufacture; clearly a sore point, given that they were in the midst of the First World War. He listed the names of some of those known to have died of a drug overdose and asked how many pilots, for example, had crashed their planes while intoxicated. His question wasn't so far-fetched. In 1907 the French navy ship *La Nive* was involved in an accident while under the command of opium-addicted officers.[30]

L'Affaire Ulmo

Drug use in the military wasn't a new thing in France. Liedekerke cites a German report from 1908 that claimed some 700 French marine officers were opium addicts; and the navy smarted for some time following the 1907 "Affaire Ulmo," in which Ulmo, a French officer and opium addict, was arrested for taking French military secrets into Germany.[31]

Leur dernière arme: Sa Majesté la Drogue! ("Their Last Weapon: Her Majesty the Drug!"). Cover of *La Grimace,* 22 July 1917. Illustration by Georges Gros.

DEUXIÈME ANNÉE N° 41   Le Numéro : 10 centimes   Dimanche 22 Juillet 1917

La Grimace

Comité de Direction :
Amédée PEYROUX
TURMEL
Charles BERNARD
députés.
& Léo POLDÈS

Hebdomadaire

SATIRIQUE, POLITIQUE, LITTÉRAIRE, THÉATRALE

Abonnement : 6 fr. par an.

Directeur Artistique :
Georges GROS

BUREAUX :
37, Rue de la Chaussée-d'Antin
Paris (IXe)
Téléph. Gutenberg 37-53

FUMERIES D'OPIUM, par Georges GROS

Leur dernière arme : Sa Majesté la Drogue !

"Eat Opium, mingle Arsenick in thy Drink.

Still thou mayst live avoiding Pen and Ink."

—John Dryden, "Absalom and Achitophel"[32]

In Britain, opium eating as a subject for writers had been exploited since the seventeenth century, notably with John Dryden writing sarcastically of fellow poet Thomas Shadwell's opium habit in "Absalom and Achitophel" (1681).[33] But it was laudanum addict Thomas De Quincey who really set the tone.

Opium smoking amongst the British literary set, however, was far less common, and included writers and artists such as Oscar Wilde, Ernest Dowson, Arthur Symons and Aubrey Beardsley. These men flaunted their decadence, experimenting with opium, absinthe and hashish.

Novelist and playwright Oscar Wilde (1854–1900) was a hit in Paris, being announced as *"le 'great event' des salons littéraires parisiennes"* of the 1891 season, and he emphasized his flamboyance by brazenly smoking opium-laced cigarettes and drinking absinthe. In Wilde's novel *The Picture of Dorian Gray* (1891), Dorian smokes opium as his life crumbles, remarking, "As long as one has this stuff, one doesn't want friends. I think I have had too many friends."[34]

Ernest Dowson (1867–1900), author of "Absinthia Taetra," an ode to absinthe, is now almost forgotten. He fell prey to absinthe and opium's charms and died a wreck at 33.

Ernest Dowson. This uncredited photograph was apparently taken during his Oxford years.

Thomas De Quincey

English author and philosopher Thomas De Quincey (1785–1859) opened the drug literature floodgates with his *Confessions of an English Opium-Eater* (1821). He was first driven to use opium because of ill health (the result of too assiduous study), a sedentary life, penury and depression. He painstakingly describes his early life, the slow inexorable descent to addiction, his literary rivalry with the poet Samuel Taylor Coleridge and his lengthy, hard-fought release after seventeen years within opium's grip. He influenced generations of writers, including Alfred de Musset, Gérard de Nerval and Charles Baudelaire, to name a few.

Imitators penned such memorable works as "An Opium-Eater in America" by William Blair (1842) and the anonymous "Confessions of a Young Lady Laudanum-Drinker" (1889).

Other British writers such as Thomas Shadwell, Wilkie Collins, the Reverend George Crabbe, Elizabeth Barrett Browning, Francis Thompson, James Thomson and John Keats were old hands when it came to experimenting or treating illness with laudanum. Morphine, more of a lady's scene and used by those who were desperate, was attractive because of its quick action. French poets Stanislas de Guaita, Edouard Dubus and Laurent Tailhade were legendary morphine addicts. Writers Guy de Maupassant and Jean Lorrain probably used it occasionally.[35]

Thomas De Quincey from *Thomas de [sic] Quincey* by Alexander H. Japp, 1890, frontispiece.

The book made it to the big screen in 1962 as *Confessions of an Opium Eater*. Set in 1890s San Francisco with Vincent Price starring as De Quincey, this movie had virtually nothing to do with the published work.

Poet Arthur Symons (1865–1945) experimented with opium, hashish and absinthe. He translated *Les Paradis artificiels* and other works of Baudelaire into English, as well as writing drug-influenced poetry, including "The Absinthe Drinker," "The Song of the Poppies" and "The Opium-Smoker."

Arthur Symons. Photograph by Frederick H. Evans from *The Poems of Arthur Symons,* 1924, frontispiece.

The Opium-Smoker

I am engulfed, and drown deliciously
Soft music like a perfume, and sweet light
Golden with audible odours exquisite,
Swathe me with cerements for eternity.
Time is no more. I pause and yet I flee.
A million ages wrap me round with night.
I drain a million ages of delight.
I hold the future in my memory.

Also I have this garret which I rent,
This bed of straw, and this that was a chair,
This worn-out body like a tattered tent,
This crust, of which the rats have eaten part,
This pipe of opium; rage, remorse, despair;
This soul at pawn and this delirious heart.[36]

Another drug-influenced English writer was Aleister Crowley (1875–1947), occultist, poet and author of the semi-autobiographical *Diary of a Drug Fiend* (1922), a novel completely concerned with the world of heroin and cocaine. Because of his bizarre and esoteric leanings—he liberally condoned Black Magic, drug use and sexual freedom—he has been largely ignored as a writer, and was, at one time, labelled "The Wickedest Man in the World." Crowley experimented with opium, ether, cocaine, hashish and morphine, and by the time he died, his daily fix of heroin would have been fatal to most addicts.[37]

Graham Greene (1904–91), whose novel *The Quiet American* (1955) reflected his own opium-smoking experiences in Indochina, wrote to his mother in 1951 telling her of his first attempt to smoke the drug and that he "rather liked it." According to his biographer Norman Sherry, Greene indulged passionately, using it as a means to overcome depression, but he never let opium take over his life.[38]

Two other British novelists who wrote about opium were Sax Rohmer and Thomas Burke; their works are discussed in the next chapter.

American authors, as a group, were not part of the opium-smoking craze; most nineteenth-century American stories that mention opium involved the world of the newly arrived Chinese. Some authors, though, like Edgar Allan Poe (1809–49), Park Barnitz (1877–1902) and Lafcadio Hearn (1850–1904), wove opium into their stories and poems.

"I had become a bounden slave in the trammels of opium, and my labors and my orders had taken a coloring from my dreams."—Edgar Allan Poe, "Ligeia" [39]

It is often assumed that Poe was an opium addict, but he almost certainly never smoked it. He allegedly made a sad and ineffective suicide attempt with laudanum, but this was an isolated incident—his poison of choice was alcohol. [40] Poe's stories reek of opium; somnolent and languid, his heroes and heroines drift through their gothic lives, beset by spectres of darkness, ghastly light, doom and despair. Direct references to opium appear in "Ligeia," "The Fall of the House of Usher," "MS Found in a Bottle" and "A Tale of the Ragged Mountains."

Little is known of Park Barnitz, poet and author of *The Book of Jade* (1901). According to a brief note by an anonymous biographer, he was a complete degenerate, doomed to an early death from neglect and use of every drug known to humankind. His poetry is wholly absorbed with death, and opium plays an integral part in his vision. [41]

Facing page, top: The "true" story of teenager Amy Burton and her descent into heroin addiction. *H is for Heroin* by David Hulburd, Popular Library, 1953.

Facing page, bottom: Although *It Ain't Hay* by David Dodge is about marijuana smuggling in San Francisco, the "hay" isn't "grass," it's money. Dell, 1946.

Below: Edgar Allan Poe. Steelplate engraving from *The Works of Edgar Allan Poe* by Richard Henry Stoddard, 1884.

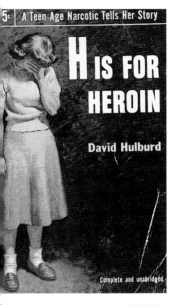

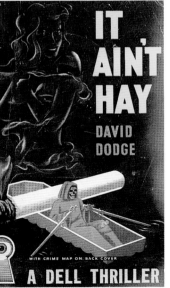

"Sure I like to watch. Sure I like to see it hit. Heroin got the drive awright—but there's not a tingle to a ton—you got to get M to get that tingle-tingle."

—Nelson Algren, *The Man with the Golden Arm*[42]

In the twentieth century, drug literature in the United States grew up alongside the criminalization of opium, morphine, heroin and cocaine. Opium, with its pipes and ritual, was too time consuming to prepare; with its telltale smoke and odour, too obvious. The cheaper, harder hitting "M" (morphine), "H" (heroin) and "C" (cocaine) took over, adding a whole new vocabulary to the already impressive lexicon of drugs. "Snow" was no longer the white stuff that fell on the ground in winter, it was the white stuff that "snow birds" snorted. "High" had nothing to do with altitude, "cold turkey" was not something found in sandwiches and "to score" did not refer to racking up points in a game.

The streetwise writing of William Burroughs's *Junkie* and *Naked Lunch,* Nelson Algren's *The Man with the Golden Arm,* William Irish's *Marijuana,* David Hulburd's *H is for Heroin,* David Dodge's *It Ain't Hay* and Frank Kane's *The Guilt Edged Frame* immortalized the language and culture of these drugs more savagely than anything that had been previously written on the subject.

CHINATOWNS

"Men and women, young girls,—virtuous or just commencing a downward career,—hardened prostitutes, representatives of the 'hoodlum' element, young clerks and errand-boys . . . and young men who had no work to do, were to be found smoking together in the back rooms of laundries in the low, pestilential dens of Chinatown, reeking with filth and overrun with vermin."—H.H. Kane, *Opium-Smoking in America and China*[1]

"The Mystery of Edwin Drood" by Gustave Doré. In 1872, Doré and Blanchard Jerrold produced a volume of sketches and observations entitled *London: A Pilgrimage*. This woodcut of an East End opium den was inspired by their visit and by Charles Dickens's unfinished novel of the same name.

Chinatowns began to appear on the west coast of North America, starting in the 1850s with the arrival of Chinese labourers at San Francisco. From California, they moved on to Portland, Seattle, Vancouver and Victoria, and later to the east coast. Primarily from the Canton area, they came with the promise of steady work in the gold fields or on the railroads, but they were paid far lower wages than whites. Poverty and racism forced them into miserable living conditions, and restrictions on bringing wives and families with them reinforced their transient existence. Similar conditions were experienced by Chinese immigrants in Australia and New Zealand.

Chinatowns rapidly became the focus of innumerable newspaper and magazine articles, social investigations, government studies and the target of countless crusades, largely because of prejudice and the opium curse.

Not that the whites didn't have their own drug problems; patent medicines containing liberal quantities of alcohol and/or opium were very popular. No one place lists all of the opium medicines that were available to the average consumer, but my impromptu survey of nostrum books, patent medicine applications and advertisements turned up well over 200. The ingredients of many patent medicines were jealously guarded, lest someone copy the formula, so many users were likely unaware that they were drugging themselves. Drug taking, whether conscious or not, was firmly ingrained in the North American psyche long before the arrival of the Chinese, and quacks continued to peddle their opiate-laced cures into the twentieth century, despite occasional scandals and investigations.

Observers have made efforts to estimate both the number of opium smokers and the number of addicts resident in Chinatowns at any given time, but the figures flung out by newspapers, crusaders and politicians seem to have no real basis in fact. In 1885, Willard B. Farwell, San Francisco's rabid anti-Chinatown reformer, tried counting bunks in the various hotels but was clearly overwhelmed by the fact that many bunks housed three or four men in constant rotation.[2]

Most accounts of nineteenth-century Chinatowns give the impression that these communities existed solely for

"Chinese Immigrants at the San Francisco Custom-House." Newspapers and journals fuelled the public's growing alarm over the numbers of Chinese immigrating into the United States. The brief article accompanying this sketch says that "John knows all the 'tricks that are vain,' and is an expert hand at eluding the vigilance of the revenue officers . . . Silks, opium, and ivory articles are generally concealed on the person of these crafty fellows, and if suspicion is aroused, they have to disrobe. The search is rigorous, and generally results in a rich harvest for the Custom-house." Cover illustration from *Harper's Weekly*, 3 February 1877. Drawing by Paul Frenzeny.

HARPER'S WEEKLY.

JOURNAL OF CIVILIZATION.

Vol. XXI.—No. 1049.]   NEW YORK, SATURDAY, FEBRUARY 3, 1877.   [WITH A SUPPLEMENT PRICE TEN CENTS.

Entered according to Act of Congress, in the Year 1877, by Harper & Brothers, in the Office of the Librarian of Congress, at Washington.

CHINESE IMMIGRANTS AT THE SAN FRANCISCO CUSTOM-HOUSE.—[See Page 91.]

the trinity of vice—drugs, prostitution and gambling. In truth, Chinatowns were complex societies, and not all residents condoned the criminal activities that took place there. And not all who took part in the gambling, whoring or opium smoking were Chinese—whites were involved as well.

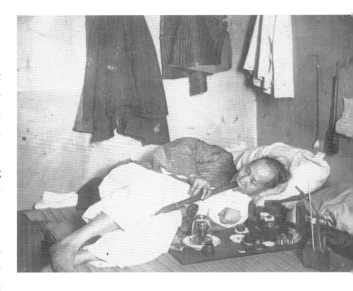

San Francisco's Chinatown was established after the arrival of the first Chinese newcomers in 1849–50, and opium soon followed. According to Richard Dillon, author of *The Hatchet Men*, 1864 was, for San Francisco, "The Year of Opium," marked by the arrival of the first large shipment of opium on the *Derby*. Customs officials found this one, but from then on were helpless against the sheer volume of opium that moved through San Francisco's port.[3] The drug was legal but subject to heavy import taxes, so successful smuggling maximized profits.

    Tours of San Francisco's opium dens became a must, attracting writers like Rudyard Kipling and Mark Twain. Twain took great pleasure in writing that "the stewing and frying of the drug and the gurgling of the juices in the stem would wellnigh turn the stomach of a statue."[4]

"Chinese Opium Fiend." Opium dens were on the San Francisco tourist track, and W., the sender of this card, wrote: "I have seen just what picture shows. It's the real thing sure." A set of scales hangs from the wall behind the smoker's head (along with what looks like a back scratcher), and a water pipe sits in the foreground, 1905.

The Night Tide

This collection of Grant Carpenter's stories, set in San Francisco, was published in 1920. In it, Fung Ching, known to his *fan quai* (white) associates as "Little Pete," finds himself the potential victim of a setup between a Jewish merchant and an undercover narcotics agent. Alarmed, he consults with his old mentor, Quan Quock Ming, who devises a plan to embarrass the agent and land the merchant in jail.

When the merchant offers to sell him opium packaged in tins, Little Pete pulls a switch, cleverly substituting similar tins and leaving the opium in the hands of the merchant. The federal agent arrests Little Pete but finds only tins of molasses and has no choice but to let him go.[5]

Chinatown Crusaders

That Chinatown was not a pretty place was confirmed by crusader Willard B. Farwell's 1885 report, which, in spite of its bigoted rhetoric, gave a frightening street-by-street picture of the poverty-stricken living conditions. He and his fellow-surveyors calculated floor space, numbers of occupants and the state of the facilities available. For example, the Palace Hotel on Jackson Street, well-known as an opium den, was home to some 400 people. The building had four privies per floor, all running into one central open drain. His report lists other buildings in similar condition, leaving out no details where smells, filth and overcrowding were concerned.[6]

By 1896 the number of opium dens in San Francisco was estimated to be in the neighbourhood of 300. Although most were in Chinatown, there were many others catering to Caucasians elsewhere in the city.

Above: "Underground Opium Den." Postcard from San Francisco, pre–1906 earthquake.

Facing page: Opium den at 614 Jackson Street, San Francisco. Taken some time before the 1906 earthquake, the caption on this postcard states that the cat has become addicted to the fumes of the drug.

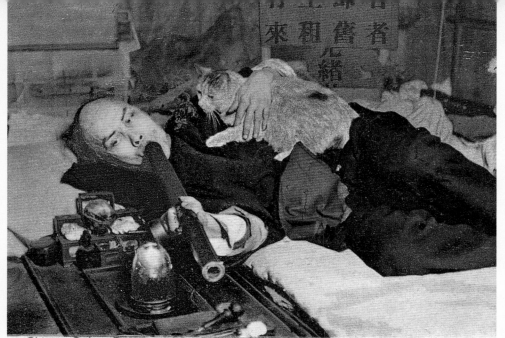

Chinese Opium Den, 614 Jackson Street, Chinatown, San Francisco; the cat has become addicted to the fumes of the drug.

"The air is thick with smoke and fetid with an indescribable odor of reeking vapors. The atmosphere is tangible. Tangible—if we may be licensed to so use the word in this instance—to four out of the five human senses. Tangible to the sight, tangible to the touch, tangible to the taste, and, oh, how tangible to the smell! You may even hear it as the opium-smoker sucks it through his pipe bowl into his tainted lungs, and you breathe it yourself as if it were of the substance and tenacity of tar. It is a sense of a horror you have never before experienced, revolting to the last degree, sickening and stupefying."—Willard B. Farwell, *The Chinese at Home and Abroad* [7]

A report quoted by Richard Dillon in *The Hatchet Men* tells of a squalid den called Blind Annie's at 718–20 Jackson Street, where women were regulars:

One of the girls volunteered that she never smoked more than twenty pills on any one visit. She explained, "That isn't enough to put me under the influence but it braces me up after a hard day and that's all I care about . . . I've hit the pipes these five years now and I'm not a fiend yet. You don't catch this girl getting to be a hophead." But as she spoke her eyelids were growing heavy. "Guess I've taken a bit too much this time," she apologized. "I'll sleep it off a bit before I go."[8]

Above: A scene from *The Dividend*, 1916. Hollywood's sensationalized portrayal of women in opium dens fuelled the outrage of righteous citizens.
Courtesy BFI Stills, Posters and Designs

Facing page: Impressions of Victoria's Chinatown. From James P. MacIntyre, "A Pacific Coast Chinatown," in *The Dominion Illustrated*, 12 September 1891.

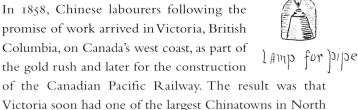

lamp for pipe

Opium pipe

In 1858, Chinese labourers following the
promise of work arrived in Victoria, British
Columbia, on Canada's west coast, as part of
the gold rush and later for the construction
of the Canadian Pacific Railway. The result was that
Victoria soon had one of the largest Chinatowns in North
America; by 1884 the city's Chinese population—15,000—
equalled that of the white
population.[9]

Victoria's Chinatown housed,
in its heyday, fourteen licensed
opium manufacturing factories, processing raw opium that
came from India via Hong Kong and San Francisco.[10] The
processed opium was sent across the country and to
the United States, usually smuggled in, not
because it was illegal but to avoid U.S. Treasury
taxes.

Victoria's fame as an opium exporting
centre was not lost on New York Chinatown
chronicler Louis J. Beck, who wrote, in 1898:

Ti Yuen, Ti Sin, Wing Chong and Quan Kai [brands of
opium]. . . come from British Columbia . . . No duty is
ever paid [as] they are smuggled into the United States
by French women, who are employed for the purpose
by the Chinese. The manufacturer in Victoria, B.C., makes a
shipment to Montreal and then the women . . . carry it over the
border.*[11]

Opium smoking

Interior of a San Francisco Chinese grocery store, undated. Although likely more elaborate than Victoria's Kwong On Lung & Co. (opposite), this store probably would also have sold opium, along with other medicines, herbs and general goods.

Victoria, B.C. July 29ᵗʰ 1885

Mᵣˢ *Tai Chung*

Bought of **Kwong On Lung & Co.**

IMPORTERS AND WHOLESALE AND RETAIL DEALERS IN

Sugar, Rice, Tea, Opium, Groceries & Provisions

CHINA PROVISIONS.

Colonist Steam Presses.

Store Street, between Cormorant and Johnson.

1885			$	c
Feb.	13	Balance due as per a/c rendered	2489	08
	19	Opium	100	00
		Salted turnips	18	00
	23	Opium	50	00
Mar.	4	China rice	525	00
	11	Opium	250	08
	17	Salted bamboo shoot		4 80
		total	3436	88
Mar.	14	Received cash	500	00
		charcoal	134	00
		Pork	100	63
			734	63
		Balance due Amount	2702	25

A running bill from the Kwong On Lung & Co. in Victoria, British Columbia, one of some fourteen factories producing opium. The 29 July 1885 invoice is made out to Mrs. Tai Chung, who ran up a tab of $3436.88 for a variety of items, including several purchases of opium.

Another city in British Columbia, Vancouver, also had a well-established Chinatown by the 1880s, located in an unhealthy, marshy area. Flimsy wooden buildings added to the neighbourhood's general air of deterioration. In 1907, the local Caucasians, incensed by what they perceived as large-scale Asian immigration, took their anger to Chinatown. The ensuing anti-Asian riot was attended by thousands who burned and looted businesses and homes.

W. L. Mackenzie King, Canada's Deputy Minister of Labour, investigated the riot and reviewed the Chinese claims for compensation for damages. Unaware of the existence of opium factories in Canada, he was shocked when the owners of two such companies presented their claims. His refusal to compensate them coincided with the formation by the Chinese of the Chinese Anti-Opium League and resulted in the passing of the Opium Act in 1908.[13] The act, drafted by King, was designed to suppress the importation of opium into Canada. Other countries were also moving to outlaw opium: China, India and Great Britain, amongst others, had already passed legislation or had legislation in the works. At the 1909 International Opium Conference held in Shanghai, representatives of thirteen governments condemned the opium industry, though their efforts had little effect.

Vancouver's Chinatown was immortalized in the 1921 rant-disguised-as-a-novel, *The Writing on the Wall,* by Hilda Glynn-Ward (1887–1966). Her scenes of opium dens stand out for their absolute excess:

Licensed Opium Factories

There were apparently as many as eight opium factories operating in Vancouver in 1888 and 1889, even though only Hip Tuck Lung and Wing Sang had obtained licences.[14]

No Opium Dens?

The following statement was included in a pamphlet produced by Quene Yip to mark Vancouver's Jubilee in 1936: "Despite assertions to the contrary, there are in Chinatown no mysterious opium dens, no underworld and no secret . . . corridors. Life . . . is peaceful and pre-eminently law-abiding."

Perhaps the opium dens were gone, but in the same year a police informer was murdered in Chinatown for his part in exposing an opium-trafficking racket a few years earlier.[15]

Judge Emily Murphy pointed an accusing finger at the ships of the Empress Steamship line, a part of the Canadian Pacific empire, used by smugglers to transport opium. In addition to the *Empress of Russia,* which Emily Murphy mentioned in her account, the Empresses of Asia, Japan, Canada and France were also used despite the efforts of CP and Canadian customs officers to stop the practice.[18] Contraband opium was tossed overboard during heavy fogs to await pickup by small boats. This postcard shows the *Empress of Japan* steaming into Vancouver harbour, undated.

The walls were lined with rows of bunks, each of which contained a corpse-like figure, stark naked, and all in different stages of the influence of the God of Narcotics. Some pulled at their long pipes, others just lay back and stared with dull, unseeing eyes at the ceiling; others again seemed quite dead . . . The floor of the den was littered with filth indescribable, and the stench of cesspools rose to meet the soul-killing fumes of opium.[16]

Mrs. Glynn-Ward's book appeared a year earlier than Judge Emily Murphy's *Black Candle,* although Judge Murphy, aka Janey Canuck, had previously written on the subject of opium in *Maclean's* magazine. Her language was as bigoted as Glynn-Ward's, but Murphy at least tried to find a solution to the spreading drug problem. Nor did she lay the blame entirely at the feet of North America's Chinese immigrants, but recognized opium as a blight that attracted every profiteer in sight. Still, she singled out Vancouver's Chinatown as a hotbed of vice.[17]

152   FRANK LESLIE'S ILLUSTRATED NEWSPAPER.   [FEB. 6, 1858.

THE OPIUM SMOKERS. DRAWN FROM LIFE.

Above: "Doesticks visits the Chinamen—Fearful effects of smoking opium upon Pelig the Sketcher." Pelig Padlin makes fun of himself in this illustration for P. B. Doesticks's article "Among the Chinamen" in *Frank Leslie's Illustrated Newspaper,* 6 February 1858, p. 152.

Left: From the same article: "The Opium Smokers. Drawn from Life."

"It was like crawling into a bottle of smoke on an exaggerated scale, for of the twenty-eight Celestials there congregated, twenty of them were smoking either opium or tobacco. The result was a cube of smoke the size of the apartment, of about the consistence [sic] of blancmange."—P. B. Doesticks, "Among the Chinamen"[19]

New York's Chinatown

By 1876, Chinatown was centred around Mott, Pell and Park, and bounded by Worth, Bayard and Bowery. Dens proliferated here and were also found on 2nd and 4th Avenues and on 23rd Street. The generally unreliable journalist P. B. Doesticks claimed there were dens at 61 Cherry and 103 James. Dens reported in the fancier parts of town included one at Cremorne Gardens on West 32nd Street and one on West 46th Street.[22]

New York's Chinatown, established possibly as early as 1858, more likely by 1876, was, perhaps more than that of any other North American city, dogged by its reputation as a centre for crime. As with other Chinatowns, it attracted its fair share of attention from police, journalists and crusaders.

H. H. Kane wrote in 1881 that opium smoking came to New York in 1876, around the same time, he claimed, that it arrived in Chicago, St. Louis and New Orleans, coinciding with Chinese migration from the west coast. His investigations of New York dens revealed Chinatown streets that were swarming "with Chinamen, Malays [and] half-breeds and a mixed tenement-house population."[20]

Louis J. Beck, in his book *New York's Chinatown* (1898), considered it better to get yellow fever than the opium-smoking habit. He described a visit to a den on West 46th Street that "at one time [was] the most luxuriously furnished joint, not only in New York, but in the United States."[21] What distinguished this particular den was its size and location: close to the heart of busy Broadway, it took up an entire three-story house. Heavy curtains shielded any

Louis J. Beck

Not much is known about author Louis J. Beck apart from a few autobiographical details supplementing his book *New York's Chinatown*. That he had a horror of the opium habit there is no doubt—he railed often against the practice within the book's pages—yet his familiarity with opium dens and the process of smoking points to thorough first-hand research.

New York's Chinatown (1898) by Louis J. Beck was illustrated with appropriate scenes right down to its decorative initial caps (facing page) for the openings to the chapters dealing with opium smoking. This page shows a scene from the luxuriously furnished West 46th Street "joint." The illustrations are probably by the author himself.

views of the interior, though according to Beck, "The furniture of the rooms was very simple—there wasn't any." Along with the scarlet-dyed mats scattered about, the rooms were "so thickly strewn with men and women that you could with difficulty make your way through the tangled feet and legs. Wallowing is the predominant posture of the opium smoker. A couch of any kind seems to be beyond his ambition."[23]

In addition to displaying his skills at journalism, fiction and sketching in his book, Beck showed his hand at verse:

The Lay of a Lotus Eater

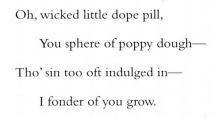

Oh, wicked little dope pill,

    You sphere of poppy dough—

Tho' sin too oft indulged in—

    I fonder of you grow.

Thou dear, diverting hop pill,

    That makes all care forgot;

Without you what would life be?

    A drear and tasteless lot.

The Tenderloin girls all love you,

    You are their heart's delight;

The sight of you brings sunshine;

    Your absence—darkest night.

A Devotee[24]

Unlike North American Chinatowns that were larger than life, Limehouse, London's East End Chinatown, and the associated opium smoking, was mainly a literary invention. Which is not to say that opium wasn't a part of the daily life of much of the population. Addiction to opium in the form of laudanum and other medicines in the British Isles reached staggering levels in the later years of the nineteenth century, particularly in the area north of Cambridge known as the "Fens."[25] As in the United States, laudanum and many other medicines like Dover's Powder, Dr. J. Collis Browne's Chlorodyne, Atkinson's Black Drop, Mrs. Winslow's Soothing Syrup and Godfrey's Cordial—to mention just a few—were also quaffed in quantity for all kinds of ills, real and imaginary. The cordials and soothing syrups were even given to teething children to sedate them; many a child's health suffered accordingly after developing an addiction to taking the stuff. Reports of death from overdose were a common feature in the "Births and Deaths" column of *The Illustrated London News.*[26]

Opium smoking, on the other hand, was confined to a higher level of society that had little to do with the ordinary opium eater, but that limited circle spawned a lurid "literary" version of Limehouse and its opium dens that blew the whole phenomenon out of proportion. Writers such as Charles Dickens, Arthur Conan Doyle and, later,

Left: Dr. J. Collis Browne's Chlorodyne. This cholera, dysentery and cough remedy contained chloral and opium. It was highly addictive.

Below: Mrs. Winslow's Soothing Syrup, advertisement. Such medicines for teething children were sold on both sides of the Atlantic. Many of these preparations contained alcohol, in addition to dangerous amounts of opium.

ADVICE TO MOTHERS
MRS. WINSLOW'S SOOTHING SYRUP
FOR CHILDREN TEETHING.

Greatly facilitates the process of Teething, by softening the gums, reducing all inflammation ; will allay ALL PAIN and spasmodic action, and is

SURE TO REGULATE THE BOWELS.

Depend upon it, Mothers, it will give rest to yourselves and

RELIEF & HEALTH TO YOUR INFANTS.

Sold by all Chemists, at 1s. 1½d. per Bottle.

Right: Dover's Powder, created by Dr. Thomas Dover (1662–1742), contained opium up into the twentieth century. This bottle, complete with original contents, likely dates from the late nineteenth century.

Sax Rohmer and Thomas Burke, portrayed Limehouse as
one of the most mysterious places on earth. Constantly
shrouded in a fog of river mist and opium smoke, the
Limehouse docklands attracted sailors, gamblers, all round
ne'er-do-wells and dope addicts from every walk of life.
Opium dens multiplied like a plague of rats, and the heart
of this pestilence supposedly was the "Chinaman" reinforced by waves of Malays, Dacoits, East Indians and
Greeks. Dens were hidden away in cavernous cellars, in
warehouses disguised as abandoned buildings, above laundries and in back of barber shops.

The sins of Limehouse threatened to spill over into the
streets of middle-class London, turning innocent but mal-
leable youths into juvenile delinquents and sweeping
society ladies into its drug-laden arms. Few writers paused
to take a realistic look at Limehouse, but Virginia Berridge,
co-author of *Opium and the People* (1981), provides statistics
to show that the Chinese population in London then was
very small, transient and quite undeserving of all of the
histrionic attention it had received. [27]

Dickens's half-finished novel, *The Mystery of Edwin
Drood* (1870), sensationalized the East End opium dens by
depicting sordid scenes involving both Caucasian and
Chinese smokers. Gustave Doré's illustration of an opium
den from his and Blanchard Jerrold's book, *London: A
Pilgrimage* (1872), inspired by *Edwin Drood,* emphasized the
subversive atmosphere, and soon the small community
grew in the public's mind to an overwhelming threat.

Edwin Drood

The Mystery of Edwin Drood opens with opium addict John Jasper, choirmaster of the Rochester cathedral, wakening to the realization that he is sharing a bed with a "Chinaman, a Lascar, and a haggard woman. The two first are in a sleep or stupor; the last is blowing at a kind of pipe, to kindle it. And as she blows, and shading it with her lean hand, concentrates its red spark of light, it serves in the dim morning as a lamp to show him what he sees of her."★

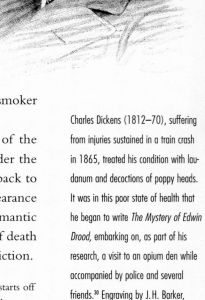

The woman is none other than " 'Er Royal Highness the Princess Puffer,"[29] ready to oblige any smoker without prejudice.

Dickens spares no mercy in his descriptions of the smokers, each of them incoherent and helpless under the effects of the drug. Jasper leaves the den and heads back to Rochester, where the mystery involving the disappearance of his nephew Edwin Drood begins in earnest. Romantic entanglements, jealousy, mesmerism and elements of death and decay obscure the meaning of Jasper's opium addiction.

★ Opium pipes are not prepared in this way (see page 66). Dickens starts off on the wrong foot with this error and goes downhill from here. There are other mistakes in this first part, but these don't interfere with the shiver of disgust the reader experiences from the general squalor of the scene.

Charles Dickens (1812–70), suffering from injuries sustained in a train crash in 1865, treated his condition with laudanum and decoctions of poppy heads. It was in this poor state of health that he began to write *The Mystery of Edwin Drood,* embarking on, as part of his research, a visit to an opium den while accompanied by police and several friends.[30] Engraving by J. H. Barker, from a photograph taken in 1868 by Mason & Co.

"In the Court." Choirmaster John Jasper wakes up and takes stock of his fellow smokers in this illustration by S. Luke Fildes from Charles Dickens's *The Mystery of Edwin Drood,* 1870, facing p. 1.

"It's opium, deary. Neither more nor less. And it's like a human creetur so far, that you can always hear what can be said against it, but seldom what can be said in its praise."—Charles Dickens, *The Mystery of Edwin Drood*[31]

Sherlock Holmes's visit in disguise to an opium den in Limehouse, an episode in the Arthur Conan Doyle (1859–1930) story "The Man with the Twisted Lip" (1887), is one of the writer's most memorable scenes. So memorable, in fact, that readers often forget that Holmes himself was not an opium addict but a cocaine addict, although he admits to taking morphine in "The Sign of the Four" (1888). Conan Doyle's imagination soars with his description of the opium den and of Holmes, who had contrived to become "very thin, very wrinkled, bent with age, an opium pipe dangling down between his knees, as though it had dropped in sheer lassitude from his fingers."[32]

Limehouse Nights (1917) by Thomas Burke (1886–1945) is a collection of stories that are loaded with atmosphere and revolve around thwarted love, revenge and opium. He wrote a number of novels set in Chinatown, as well as nonfiction books about London's colourful history.

Sax Rohmer (1883–1959), the pen name of Arthur Ward, became synonymous with Limehouse, "the Yellow Peril," Fu Manchu and opium.

Rohmer's sensational novels such as *Dope, The Yellow Claw* and the Fu-Manchu series *(Fu-Manchu's Bride, The Insidious Dr. Fu-Manchu, The Hand of Fu-Manchu)* captivated generations of readers, shocking them with tales of sorcery, corruption and adventure. No matter where his mysteries were set, whether they took place in England, the south of France or Egypt, he worked in at least some mention of that infamous hellhole known as Limehouse.

Spoiling Our Illusions

Thomas Burke wrote a number of books about London. In one of them, *Nights in London,* he tried to destroy Limehouse's reputation for danger and opium: "Taking a jolt of 'chandu' in a Limehouse room is about as exciting as taking a mixed vermuth [sic] at the Leicester Lounge . . . One has read, in periodicals, of the well-to-do people from the western end, who hire rooms here and come down, from time to time, for an orgy. That is another story for the nursery."[33]

Turn-of-the-century tourists could confidently navigate the streets of Limehouse armed with their Baedeker map. From *Baedeker's London and Its Environs,* 1900.

Limehouse Streets

The Limehouse of legend covered an area of East London that included Limehouse Causeway, Ratcliffe Highway, Commercial Road, Pennyfields, West India Dock Road and Pekin Street.

Thomas Burke's story "The Chink and the Child," published in his book *Limehouse Nights,* is about Cheng Huan, who has found himself washed up on the streets of foul and fetid Limehouse. He falls hopelessly in love with twelve-year-old Lucy, daughter of the violent Battling Burrows.

Cheng meets her in an opium den where "the dirt of years, tobacco of many growings, opium, betel nut, and moist flesh allied themselves in one grand assault against the nostrils."[34] Setting aside the fact that Lucy is but twelve years old, the reader is almost relieved when Cheng takes

her to his own squalid digs and they become lovers. Battling, having discovered that "a yellow man is after his kid," recaptures her, and beats her to death. To avenge her, Cheng kills him by leaving a deadly snake in the house.

D.W. Griffiths's silent film *Broken Blossoms* (1919), based on "The Chink and the Child," stars Lillian Gish as Lucy, Richard Barthelmess as Cheng Huan and Donald Crisp as Battling Burrows. True to the story, except in the manner of Cheng's revenge, the film was a great success.

Opium and Limehouse

Other stories in *Limehouse Nights* that mention opium are "Tai-fu and Pansy Greer," "The Gorilla and the Girl," "Gracie Goodnight" and "The Paw."

Richard Barthelmess in the role of Cheng Huan in D.W. Griffith's movie *Broken Blossoms* (U.S. 1919).

Facing page: Mahlon Blaine's illustration for Thomas Burke's 1917 story "The Chink and the Child." From *Limehouse Nights,* 1926, frontispiece.

"O li'l Lucia .... White Blossom .... Twelve years old!"

Opium Goes to the Movies

The public was entertained by
numerous movies with Chinese
themes. Opium smoking or drug
addiction was often part of the
stories, as in this movie *The Man
Who Came Back* (U.S. 1930),
about a man who finds his drug-
addicted girlfriend in Hong
Kong. Starring Janet Gaynor,
Charles Farrell, Kenneth
MacKenna and William Holden,
and directed by Raoul Walsh, it
was based on a play by Jules
Eckert Goodman. Other movies
of note involving opium include
The Letter (U.S. 1940), set in
Southeast Asia, with Bette Davis
and Herbert Marshall, based on a
story by W. Somerset Maugham;
Charlie Chan in Shanghai (U.S.
1935), with Warner Oland as
Charlie Chan investigating an
opium ring; and *Drifting* (U.S.
1923), about opium smuggling in
China, with Anna May Wong,
Matt Moore and Priscilla Dean.

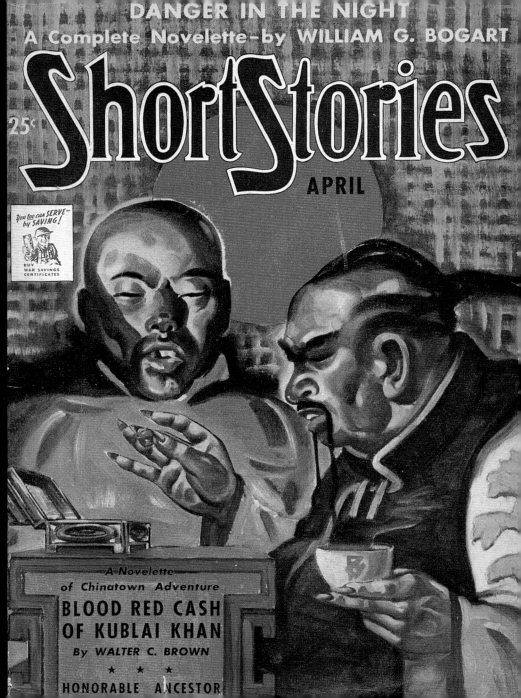

OPIUM HITS THE STREET

Crime Takes Over

Opium, morphine and heroin were avidly adopted by twentieth-century crime writers. Featured in magazines such as *Short Stories* (opposite), *Real Detective* and *Dime Detective,* the lingo and mannerisms of opium dealers and users entered the mainstream.

"Blood Red Cash of Kublai Khan." Master Crook Eric Meister kills the owner of the three blood-red jade cash, or disks, that carry the seal of Kublai Khan, by doping his tea with opiates, in Walter C. Brown's tale of a Chinatown murder. *Short Stories*, April 1943. "Chinatown Always Looked Like a Pushover—Till You Start Pushing!"

"1,500,000 DRUG USERS IN AMERICA, HE SAYS"—*New York Times,* 14 May 1923[1]

During the long history of opium's voyage around the world, fabulous fortunes accrued to some, but the futures of untold numbers of wretches were destroyed. As opium use grew to alarming proportions, frantic headlines magnified the problem; conferences were held, imports were halted, smuggling increased and eventually anti-drug laws were passed. In the course of a few decades, taking opium changed from an exotic if legal vice to a criminal activity run by gangs selling drugs on the streets.

Towards the end of the nineteenth century, numbers of addicts wandered about, helpless; they were treated as insane, ill, criminal, depraved or mentally deficient. The clinics that were opened to help them were so swamped and could do so little that they quickly closed, leaving the desperate habitués to fend for themselves once again. Their plight further fuelled efforts by anti-drug crusaders in

Britain and China, in particular; by the early twentieth century they forced governments to heed demands calling for a halt to the opium trade. Although Britain continued to profit from the sale of opium to China, the House of Commons found the issue morally troubling and finally signed a treaty with the Chinese in 1906–7, resolving to eradicate "the evils arising from foreign and native opium."[2]

France, like Britain, faced the dilemma of condoning the opium trade in its colony of Indochina while trying to restrict domestic use. After 1908, opium in France could theoretically be purchased only from a pharmacy and only with a prescription signed by a doctor. In 1909, an effort was made to close down opium dens.[3]

On February 1, 1909, the first International Opium Conference at Shanghai was held; then a second (1912) and a third (1914) in The Hague were convened, calling for stricter control of opiates—including opium, morphine and heroin—and a licensing system for medical use. These conferences, and others, led individual countries to draft restrictive legislation against the traffic in drugs. In 1908, Britain passed the Poisons and Pharmacy Act; in 1909, the United States enacted the Smoking Opium Exclusion Act; and in 1911, Canada introduced the Opium and Narcotic Drug Act to stiffen penalties for narcotic use under the existing Opium Act of 1908.[4]

Tough new laws were also being passed in Asia: for example, in 1910, Hong Kong officially called for the closing of opium dens and imposed heavy fines on those caught

Not Wanted in the Asylum

The *Sixth Biennial Report of the Oregon State Insane Asylum for 1895* complained that the largest number of escapees were the opium-addicted inmates. They argued that these addicts and other inebriates were "undesirable elements, not proper subjects for treatment at the asylum." For the two years covered by the report, 41 of the 632 patients admitted were opium addicts.[5]

Facing page: United States Treasury Department, Internal Revenue Order Form. Following the passage of the 1914 Harrison Narcotic Act, federal drug legislation made opiate trafficking a major offence. Pharmacists and doctors were required to register with the Department of the Treasury, pay taxes and keep records of narcotics dispensed.[6]

TREASURY DEPARTMENT

ORIGINAL
Value One (1) Cent

UNITED STATES INTERNAL REVENUE ORDER FORM FOR OPIUM OR COCA LEAVES, OR COMPOUNDS, MANUFACTURES, SALTS, DERIVATIVES OR PREPARATIONS THEREOF UNDER SECTION 2 OF THE ACT OF CONGRESS, APPROVED DECEMBER 17, 1914.

SERIES OF 1923

Special tax under said Act in each of the classes and at the location specified below must be paid for a fiscal period covering the date inserted by the purchaser before this form may be used.

NO. DD53397 **DATE** Feb 6th 1926

TO BE FILLED IN BY PURCHASER

THIS ORDER IS FOR EXACTLY 3 **ITEMS.**

NUMBER OF ITEMS MUST BE SPECIFIED BY PURCHASER OR FORM RETURNED

Unless this order calls only for one ounce of an aqueous narcotic solution, it may be filled only by an importer, manufacturer, producer, compounder, or wholesale dealer (a class 1 or 2 registrant); if filled by any other person, liability to tax under the Act as a producer will be incurred by the vendor if broken or unstamped packages are supplied, and liability to tax thereunder as a wholesale dealer will be similarly incurred if stamped packages are furnished.

The merchandise requested below may not be furnished if this form shows any alteration or erasure or evidence of any change whatsoever.

If unused upon discontinuance of business this form must be returned for cancellation to the collector who issued it.

NAME, ADDRESS, REGISTRY AND CLASS NUMBERS, AND DATE TO BE INSERTED IN COLLECTOR'S OFFICE

2939

Jas M Miller
Crockett Va

CLASS 4 **DIST. OF VA.**

ISSUED JAN 30 924 **BY** J. C. NOEL

DATE — COLLECTOR

To Jas. M. Miller

STREET **CITY** Wytheville **STATE** Va

You are requested to send to me at the location above specified by the collector of internal revenue for this district the following merchandise which comes within the purview of the act of December 17, 1914, as amended by the act of November 23, 1921, for use, sale, or distribution in the lawful conduct of my business or legitimate practice of my profession, for which I am duly registered under the above stated registry number at this time under said Act, and for which I have paid the taxes necessary to qualify me in the above stated classes for a fiscal period covering the date of this order which has been inserted above by me:

TO BE FILLED IN BY PURCHASER

ITEM	CATALOGUE NUMBER IF ANY	NUMBER OF PACKAGES	SIZE OF PACKAGE NUMBER OF POUNDS, OUNCES, GRAINS, PILLS, TABLETS, ETC., IN EACH PACKAGE	NAME OF ARTICLE NAME OF NARCOTIC DRUG INVOLVED MUST BE STATED	NUMBER OF STAMPED PACKAGES FURNISHED	DATE FILLED
1			5-00 1/4 gr	Mor. Sul. Tab tril		
2			200	mor sul 1/4 gr Atropine 1/150 hyp podermic		
3			500	After pain tab mor sul 1/10		
4						
5						
6				Void 3/15/26		
7						
8						
9						
10						

H. S. McAULEY FEDERAL AGENT

NAME OF PERSON OR FIRM IF NOT AN INDIVIDUAL

Jas. M. Miller

SIGNATURE OF PURCHASER, OR HIS ATTORNEY OR AGENT

operating, found in, or escaping from a den.[7] But lax enforcement remained a stumbling block, so opium smoking carried on relatively unhindered throughout Asia and morphine injecting rose, exacerbated by the flooding of cheap morphine into China, one feature of Japan's involvement in the drug trade.

OPIUM HABIT

CURED Painlessly at home by one who has had SEVENTEEN YEARS' PRACTICE in treating and curing this disease. For full particulars send for **THE TEST OF TIME** containing testimonials of hundreds who have been permanently cured. Address, **DR. S. B. COLLINS, La Porte, Ind.**

Above and background: The secret to "curing" the opium habit painlessly was to get hooked on something else. Opium habit cures, for opium smokers or laudanum drinkers, often contained morphine. Advertisements promising cures for other weaknesses such as alcoholism or the tobacco habit also abounded.

Now that Britain was out of the picture, the Japanese, first with their occupation of Formosa (Taiwan) in 1895, then of portions of northern and coastal China by 1918, became a supplier of opium and morphine to the Chinese. Japan had purchased no opium from India until 1911–12 when it bought £76,8117 worth. The next year it bought £129,545 worth. In 1911, Japan also purchased 5½ tons of medical morphine from Britain; by 1920 this had risen to 20 tons, the bulk of which, it seems, went directly to China.[8]

Morphine, which had been introduced into China in the late nineteenth century, was at first lauded by missionaries and addicts alike as a potential cure for the opium-smoking habit. Pills containing opium or morphine were handed out by missionaries—particularly ones with a medical background—with such regularity that they were called "Jesus opium." A survey undertaken by the 1912 Conference on Opium listed some ninety brands of anti-opium pills; most of them contained morphine.[9] The search for a cure had in fact introduced a new fiend.

Le Gang de l'opium (The Opium Gang).
A pamphlet-length police thriller by
Charles Richebourg, Paris, 1956.

Morphine cures for the opium habit were sold in North America as well, advertised in newspapers and magazines. However, the wording of both ads and packaging seldom mentioned the nature of the ingredients.

In 1906, coincident with the passing of the U.S. Pure Food and Drug Act, which specified that medicine labels must state narcotic content and prohibited false or misleading claims, *Collier's* magazine ran a series exposing the fraudulent patent medicine industry, highlighting the dangers of these over-the-counter medicines. Large-scale confiscations and sensational displays of the destruction of opium and pipes further publicized government efforts to wipe out the habit.[10] Citizens had fewer excuses to plead ignorance.

By the 1920s, widespread adoption of anti-opium and anti-drug legislation had put opium out of reach of the ordinary person. No longer available without a prescription, opium and morphine became forbidden stuff, and as such the centre of an emerging criminal class and the streetwise drug pusher.

As the *raison d'être* of criminal activity, opium—and its derivatives morphine and heroin—took on a new persona, ensuring the end of lazy hours spent in smoke-filled dens. Violence, gang warfare and smuggling escalated on an international scale, and, in spite of government and individual efforts to find solutions, little has changed; these problems are still with us.

LES ROUTES DU POISON

On peut, à l'heure qu'il est, noir où les rivières creusent leur lit.

RUSSEL PACHA.

PRENEZ la carte du monde. Sur cette carte, entourez d'un trait rouge Istamboul et Sofia, d'une part ; Marseille, Paris, Le Havre, Vienne, Berlin, Hambourg, New-York, d'autre part. Soulignez encore là-bas, les mers de Chine, Osaka, Changhaï, Tien-tsin et Daïren. N'oubliez pas non plus Alexandrie, Port-Saïd, Smyrne, Le Pirée, Trieste et Barcelone. Reliez d'un pointillé toutes ces villes.

Vous aurez ainsi tracé le réseau des routes du poison.

Entendez-moi, je ne veux pas dire que l'affaire est aussi simple et que la drogue suive d'approvisionnement les marchés illicites suive aussi fidèlement les routes ainsi tracées.

A vouer qu'il m'ait fallu pour bien le regard s'y repose un instant.

Du Japon à New-York, en passant par Marseille ! Des gratte-ciels de Broadway aux plaines de Mandchourie ! Des docks de Hambourg aux pyramides d'Égypte ! Du Bosphore aux Champs-Élysées ! Il y en a pour tous les goûts. Le décor est vaste comme l'univers.

Animez maintenant ce fameux choix d'images des noms magiques de l'âge moderne : export, import, ordre, connaissements, factures, télégrammes, banques, places et téléphone ! Tout cela ici trouvera sa place.

Bateaux, wagons-lits et avions ne seront pas de trop non plus. Tout ce qui circule dans l'espace, tout ce qui relie les pays entre eux, par-dessus les frontières, va s'être utilisé ; ce grand paquebot relié et blanc qui remonte la Mer Rouge ; ce rapide aux voitures bleues qui longe, en Bulgarie, le défilé de la Nichava ; cet avion qui survole les flèches du diamètre de Strasbourg ; cette vedette rapide qui, tous feux éteints, glisse sur les eaux endormies...

Est-ce tout ? Non pas. Vous allez omettre le plus important de l'affaire : le code secret.

Le télégraphe transmet son hiéroglyphe :

ARCWY YHXED CLASC

lisez :

Marchandises renfermées dans les caisses Nᵒˢ 3 et 4.

Si vous tombez en arrêt devant ces chiffres : 76.010 et 75.379, traduisez : *Par mer, voie de Port-Saïd.*

et

Black (opium) de Constantinople.

Tel est, j'ose dire, le matériel.

Il y manque encore les chaînons de l'engrenage. Les voici : ils sont de toute grosseur, de tout acabit.

Si ce gangster de la drogue descend dans des palaces, voyage en pullman et possède un yacht de plaisance, le convoyeur du poison peut-être cet homme qui, dans les flancs du navire, graisse les machines, ou ce stewart en veste blanche qui sert, au bar, des boissons glacées.

Si cet important trafiquant de stupéfiants

(1) Voir à *Détective* 2, depuis le nᵒ 239.

traite à Paris les gros achats de morphine et d'héroïne qui doivent être secrètement livrés à New-York, cet autre n'a peut-être pour mission que de recruter les complices (douaniers ou navigateurs) du transport clandestin.

Si celui-ci est le chef, ceux-là ne sont que d'obscurs comparses qui, le plus souvent, ignorent le nom de l'homme qui les dirige et qui, pourtant, exécutent, point par point, les consignes reçues.

Si cette bande accapare le marché de la coco en Europe, cette autre, sa rivale, alimente d'héroïne l'Extrême-Orient ; cette troisième, les États-Unis.

Si le trafic international a, ici, aujourd'hui, son quartier général, ses repaires, ses arsenaux, ses sites de guerre, demain c'est là qu'un nouveau centre mondial se sera reconstitué.

Il faudra modifier la carte, y tracer de nouvelles lignes, mais les rouges, les ramifications du formidable réseau resteront les mêmes.

Et les Usines de Rêve domineront à nouveau l'inquiétant panorama des routes de la drogue.

◆ ◆ ◆

Ce n'est pas sans peine que j'ai pu suivre la trace toujours fuyante de ces chemins mystérieux. Ce n'est pas en un jour que j'ai pu pénétrer l'énigme de l'extraordinaire organisation qui se cache derrière la vente au détail du moindre gramme d'héroïne et de cocaïne. Il me fallut, sans me lasser, parcourir bien des étapes, surmonter bien des obstacles.

— Et moi ! me disait-on, vous avez la trace du poison ! Vous avez là au point le plus délicat du problème. Si déjà, lors de mes premières recherches, je n'avais rencontré que méfiance et réticences, une étrange réserve accueillait à nouveau mes questions.

Des noms, parfois, échappaient à mes interlocuteurs, des noms de grands seigneurs de la drogue, mais si furtivement qu'il m'était impossible de les lier entre eux, de les situer dans ce réseau qui, du bassin méditerranéen, s'étend au monde entier.

Mustapha lui-même, mon providentiel ami, semblait frappé soudain d'amnésie et limitait ses propos à de vagues considérations.

Ainsi, le voile qui s'était un moment entr'ouvert était retombé. J'étais de nouveau dans une impasse.

Ce fut le moment qu'une singulière proposition me parvint.

On m'avait, ce jour-là, présenté un haut fonctionnaire de Stamboul.

— Je sais ce que vous cherchez, me dit ce personnage. Et je vous offre à vous faire... La police turque est actuellement sur la piste d'une bande qui cherche à liquider un gros stock d'héroïne. Nous avons déjà avancé pas mal d'argent à des intermédiaires. Il ne nous manque plus

que le gros acheteur arrivant de l'étranger. Nous avons songé à vous...

— Mais, dis-je lorsque j'eus surmonté ma surprise, vous oubliez que j'entends me borner à mon rôle de reporter et que, d'ailleurs, la bande dont vous me parlez ne me traitera pas longtemps à me démasquer.

— Nous ferons savoir que c'est sous le couvert de la profession de journaliste que vous êtes venu ici traiter une affaire d'héroïne. Si vous réussissez, c'est un grand service que vous rendrez à la Turquie dans la lutte contre les stupéfiants. Nous enverrons avec vous l'un de nos émissaires à l'enrichir.

Ayant conclu, avec de gros fournisseurs de cocaïne, une affaire d'un million et demi, il demanda à les clients de l'accompagner en Allemagne pour y prendre livraison de la drogue. Le retour s'effectua dans une vieille voiture de location. Peu avant la frontière, la voiture stoppa.

— Descendez, fit Gourevidès à ses clients. Il faut que je m'arrange avec les douaniers. Vous me rejoindrez après.

Les trafiquants débarquèrent et attendi-

votre hôtel. Si vous acceptez, il vous donnera la marche à suivre. A demain, monsieur ; nous attendons votre réponse.

Je préparais que je fusse à me m'étonner de rien, je me retrouvai dans la rue sans avoir à la force d'articuler un mot. Quelle singulière stupéfiante proposition ! Pourquoi choisir, pour tendre ce périlleux traquenard, une personne que nous n'étions au courant de moi des secrets du trafic ?

Je dormis guère cette nuit-là. Et, le lendemain, lorsque l'émissaire se présenta à l'heure dite, mon parti était pris...

L'émissaire était une jeune fille, dont le bas du visage était dissimulé sous un grand col de fourrure. Elle m'adressa de signe convenu et nous montâmes dans un taxi qui fila vers les quais de Galata.

— Où allons-nous ?

— Je ne sais pas. J'ai seulement pour mission de vous accompagner et de vous servir d'interprète.

Un homme, dans l'arrière-salle d'un café, nous attendait.

Il y eut, entre la jeune fille et lui, une longue conciliante. Jamais, depuis le début de mon aventureux voyage, je n'avais senti peser sur moi une si lourde angoisse.

— On vous fait dire que l'interprète, que vous n'avez rien à craindre, que l'homme ne pourra soupçonner que vous n'êtes pas réellement un acheteur et que la bande a un besoin d'argent qu'elle conclura l'affaire sans trop y regarder.

— Je veux croire, répondis-je, que vous avez dans votre plan toutes vos responsabilités. Cependant, je refuse. Le rôle que vous voulez me faire jouer n'est pas compatible avec mon état de reporter. Si je ne puis jouer l'aventurer véreux, tant pis...

L'interprète rapporta ma réponse. L'homme hocha la tête et se leva, l'air soucieux.

— Tant pis ! répéta la jeune fille.

Nous nous quittâmes sur ce bref entretien. Je me sentais à la bande de la drogue où vous êtes aventuré, toute légèreté, toute imprudence n'allait-elle pas me rendre suspect à mon tour ?

J'en étais là de mes réflexions, lorsque, remontant la rue de Péra, je sentis soudain qu'on me frappait à l'épaule. Je me retournai. Mustapha me plantait devant moi, m'offrit une cigarette et, d'une voix tranquille :

— Vous avez eu raison, me dit-il, de refuser. Dans le monde de la drogue où vous êtes aventuré, toute légèreté, toute imprudence.....

L'Américain Del Gracio, l'un des maîtres du marché illicite de la drogue New-York.

Les initiales M. et H. désignent, sur cette lettre, morphine et héroïne.

peut prévoir les conséquences... Souvenez-vous-en.

◆ ◆ ◆

Je n'ai jamais su ni ce qui s'était passé, ni quelle sorte d'épreuve j'avais pu, ainsi, subir à mon insu, ni quel avait été le véritable instigateur de l'inexplicable complot ; mais le souvenir de l'étrange entrevue m'a toujours dominé, lorsque, plus tard, voyant plus clair sur ma route, j'ai patiemment reconstitué les grands épisodes de cette lutte gigantesque dans les années qui succédèrent à la guerre, et l'attrait, pour les trafiquants, des énormes bénéfices du commerce illicite des stupéfiants.

Pour profiter d'une situation aussi exceptionnelle, il fallait des hommes exceptionnels.

Ce sont des Grecs qui, d'abord, comprirent tout le parti qu'on pouvait tirer, avant que tout obstacles eussent surgi, d'un trafic aussi fructueux.

Le premier groupement connu est celui des frères Eliopoulos, dont le principal lieutenant était un certain David Gourevidès ou Gourevitché.

Le groupement devait rapidement devenir l'un des maîtres du marché mondial.

Les débuts avaient été obscurs.

Seul, Gourevidès avait déjà mesuré sa force dans un coup d'audace qui devait commencer à l'enrichir.

rent. Soudain, le bruit d'une explosion les fit se retourner. Près de la voiture en flammes, Gourevidès agitait des bras désespérés.

— Un accident, bégayait-il ; la cameleote est fichue.

On ouvrit la valise. Elle était vide. Le contenu s'était volatilisé dans l'explosion.

— Messieurs, gémit Gourevidès, parjurons les dégâts de cette mésaventure. Je vais vous rembourser la moitié de l'argent que vous m'avez remis : voici sept cent cinquante mille francs.

Les marchands, médusés, acceptèrent.

Gourevidès garda l'autre moitié et, lorsqu'il fut seul, se frotta les mains. Le tour était bien joué. La valise qui contenait la drogue avait été, au moment de l'incendie volontaire de la voiture, remplacée par la sienne.

Cela se passait en 1927.

C'est alors qu'un ancien fournisseur ruiné de l'armée grecque, Élie Eliopoulos, songea à réédifier sa fortune en s'occupant, à son tour, du trafic des stupéfiants.

Chassé de St... (en bas) le cent... dial du trafi... réorganisa à S... haut) mais les... cations du fou... réseau sont les...

Gourevidès fut de campagne. L'homme ses appétits.

— Allons en Chi à ramasser la dos...

Eliopoulos et Go Changhaï, pour un reprirent une sec trême-Orient ; un certain à Tientsin, un certai s'ils revinrent à Pa n'était à la besogne.

Il ne s'agissait p ver la drogue à ex fonctionnait sur la monopole de l'État... nirent. Aucun obst... ficat de douane, de gramme n'était ver consommation loca qu'en Chine, la drog dissimulée dans d'...

L'or afflux, Eliop... organisa sa bande illicite. Mais on p... pais décidait, en fabriques de drogue certaines, le group... ser les courtiers et sion de ses mesur faire sentir sur tou...

Eliopoulos songea... porter ailleurs ses Usines du Rêve à r à Stambou...

L'une d'elles, s'... coundjouk, sous la... Mechehaler, les dis qui le permis de fa... au gouvernement...

Eliopoulos décid... Turquie. Mais il n'e... désormais, se tenir grands seigneurs d... dean Isaac-Astruc, premières rivé d'espionnage... se faire s... Chag... bande... Cha...

DÉTECTIVE

Les routes du poison

commissionnaires, ses chefs d'entrepôt, ses courtiers, ses hommes de main.

Chaque homme de main allait avoir à sa solde tout un réseau de complices recrutés dans les ports, sur les bateaux, dans les trains.

L'argent affluait, mais les cupidités allaient s'aiguiser. Parvenues au faîte de leur prospérité, les deux fabriques de Stamboul, celle du Bosphore et celle d'Eyoub, allaient devenir deux forteresses rivales.

Et, sur les routes du poison, les trafiquants enrichis, grisés par leur fortune trop rapide, allaient se guetter, s'espionner et chercher à se ravir les grands marchés de la drogue.

◼ ◼ ◼

Quel impressionnant chassé-croisé! Quelle ruée vers l'or! C'est à qui arrivera le premier pour prendre sa part dans cette dangereuse épidémie...

De 1917 à 1930, l'héroïne afflue d'Europe en Chine par les ports de Changhaï, de Tien-tsin et de Dairen. Mais le Japon joue des coudes et, bientôt, s'en mêle. Expédiant à son tour de la drogue, il fera baisser les prix. Les chimistes nippons iront monter leurs fabriques jusqu'en Mandchourie.

En 1929, les fabriques de France commencent à ralentir leurs envois. Aussitôt, les Usines de Rêve de Stamboul leur succèdent et expédient mensuellement à la Chine près de deux tonnes d'héroïne et de base morphine. Les fabriques turques ferment, les usines chinoises redoublent d'efforts.

Voici maintenant Sofia et ses fabriques au centre du marché mondial ! Voici l'héroïne expédiée sur Hambourg pour le marché amé-

Tout va être utilisé — ce train de luxe, cet avion, ce paquebot — sur les routes du poison qui sillonnent le monde jusqu'en Extrême-Orient

Entre l'opium «littéraire», entre les esclaves de la drogue et les Usines de Rêve, sait-on quel formidable réseau représentent, à travers le monde, les routes qui charrient la poudre folle?
(Lire, pages 8 et 9, la suite des révélations sensationnelles de Marcel Montarron.)

Et d'obscurs comparses qui ignorent le nom du chef qui les dirige seront recrutés dans les ports par les hommes de train des seigneurs de la drogue.

ricain, et sur Marseille pour les marchés d'Égypte et d'Extrême-Orient...

Mais l'opium bulgare s'épuise.

C'est la Turquie qui doit fournir la matière première.

Les trafiquants nourriront de nouveaux espoirs, les cupidités renaissent, les chantages aussi...

Demain, jusqu'où conduiront les routes qui charrient la poudre folle !...

(A suivre.)   Marcel MONTARRON

Jeudi prochain :

**CHEZ UN ROI
DE LA CONTREBANDE**

In this edition of *Détective,* a French weekly police magazine, the languid reader is deep into Jean Cocteau's *Opium.* The article "Usines de Rêve" ("Dream Factories") by Marcel Montarron is a whirlwind tour of the drug underground, filled with tales of secret codes, gangsters' yachts, books stuffed with heroin and clandestine meetings with young women at the Istanbul port of Galata. In one paragraph Montarron summarizes the vast network: "From Japan to New York, passing en route through Marseille! From the sky scrapers of Broadway to the plains of Manchuria! From the docks of Hamburg to the pyramids of Egypt! From the Bosphorus to the Champs-Elysées! There's something for all tastes."[11]

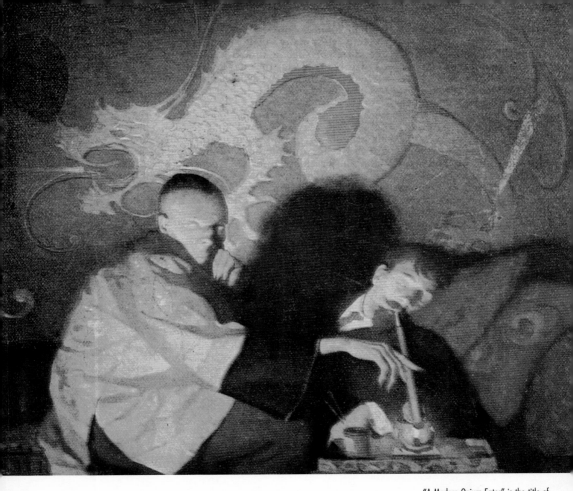

"A Modern Opium Eater" is the title of the story which accompanied this N.C. Wyeth painting. Wyeth apparently researched the painting by visiting an opium den in Philadelphia.[1] The article was written by anonymous journalist No. 6606 and was published in *The American Magazine,* June 1914.

NOTES

Front Matter

1   Brownlow, 1990, 108.

Introduction

1   Malraux, 1934 (1933), 357. The
     quote is from the opium addict
     Old Gisors.
2   De Quincey, 1902 (1821), 194.
3   *The Family Physician,* c. 1900, 158.
4   De Quincey, 1902 (1821), 181;
     Berridge, 1981, xxi; and Lewin,
     1964 (1931), 30–31.
5   Anonymous, 1844, 60.
6   *The Illustrated London News,* 25
     August 1860, 180.
7   Kipling, 1910, 52.

The Drowsy Poppy

1   Farrère, 1904, 256.
2   Merlin, 1984, 29.
3   Barnitz, 1901, 44.
4   Kapoor, 1995, 22–23.
5   Merlin, 1984, 211.
6   Gunther, 1959 (1933), 456–60;
     and Pliny, 1856, 275–76, 300.
7   Ovid, 1990, 85, lines 99,100.
8   Merlin, 1984, 222.
9   Homer, 1946, 70; and Merlin,
     1984, 215.
10   Ovid, 1958, book XI, 317.
11   Ovid, 1951, iv, lines 661–62; and
     Virgil, 1981, iv, lines 481–82.

12   Bachmann and Coppel, 1989, 98.
13   Goldsmith, 1939, 107.
14   Thomson, 1876, 147.
15   "Opium" in The *New
     Encyclopedia Britannica,* 1985, 508.
16   Bachmann and Coppel, 1989, 108.
17   Kipling, 1910, 433.
18   Ibid., 435.
19   "The traffic in opium carried on
     with China," *The Chinese
     Repository,* April 1837, 552.
20   Kipling, 1910, 437.
21   Williams, 1899, 376.
22   Whitaker, 1879.
23   "Opium," *Encyclopædia
     Britannica,* 1878, 82.
24   Kipling, 1910, 437.
25   "Articles of Import and Export
     of Canton," *The Chinese
     Repository,* 1834, 467.
26   *Murray's Handbook to India, Burma
     & Ceylon,* 1909, 90.
27   "Opium," *Encyclopædia
     Britannica,* 1878, 811–14.
28   Burton, 1927 (1621), 593 (Garcias
     ab Horto is more commonly
     known as Garcia da Orta);
     Pomet, 1712 (1694), 216–17; and
     de Amicis, 1896, 125.
29   Gautier, 1857, 120.
30   Rush, 1990, 1; Honoré, 1896, 174;
     and Trocki, 1990, 2.

31   The quote and the description of
     the process are from Honoré,
     1896, 174–75.

Opium and the East

1   Magre, 1922, 62.
2   Barbosa, 1866, 27–28, 60, 300.
3   Goldsmith, 1939, 44.
4   Collis, 1968 (1946), 3 and 5.
5   Watney, 1974, 121.
6   Goldsmith, 1939, 40; and
     Edkins, 1898, 9.
7   Edkins, 1898, 9 and 14.
8   Goldsmith, 1939, 41; and Edkins,
     1898, 41 and 43–44.
9   Williams, 1899, 377.
10   Collis, 1968 (1946), 5.
11   "The traffic in opium carried on
     with China," *The Chinese
     Repository,* April 1837, 547.
12   "Articles of Import and Export
     of Canton," *The Chinese Repository,*
     1834, 467; and Huc, 1859, 19.
13   Tang, "Proclamation respecting
     opium," *The Chinese Repository,*
     1839, 499. Tang was the governor
     of Kwangtun and Kwangse.
14   Cited in Williams, 1899, 378.
15   Waley, 1958, 33.
16   Collis, 1968 (1946), 46; and
     Heu-Kew, *The Chinese Repository,*
     1837, 399.

17 Williams, 1899, 378.

18 Edkins, 1898, 49–50.

19 Collis, 1968 (1946), 42.

20 Collis, 1968 (1946), 38; and Fortune, 1847, 139–41.

21 Collis, 1968 (1946), 43–45.

22 Ibid., 44.

23 "Opium," *The Chinese Repository,* 1832, 159.

24 Edkins, 1898, 44.

25 Williams, 1899, 487–48.

26 "Opium, opium dealers and smokers," *The Chinese Repository,* 1838, 392.

27 Lubbock, 1914, 4; and Hwang Tseôtsze, *The Chinese Repository,* 1838, 273.

28 Williams, 1899, 498–501.

29 Williams, 1899, 503; "Crisis in the opium traffic," *The Chinese Repository,* 1839, 70; Waley, 1958, 34, 55; and Collis, 1968 (1946), 22.

30 Waley, 1958, 11.

31 Lin, *The Chinese Repository,* 1839, 9–12; and Waley, 1958, 93.

32 Williams, 1899, 510.

33 Collis, 1968 (1946), 219; "Crisis in the opium traffic," *The Chinese Repository,* 1839, 72–76; and "Opium," in *Encyclopædia Britannica,* 1878, 813.

34 Williams, 1899, 549.

35 Eden, 1877, 90.

36 Richthofen, 1903, 153.

37 "Expenses of the War With China," *The Illustrated London News,* 21 July 1860, 56.

38 "Opium in the Army," *The Chinese Repository,* 1832, 31.

39 Unnamed source, quoted in Murphy, 1922, 293.

40 Lawrence, 1870, 238–39.

41 Sirr, 1849, 3.

42 Ibid., 251.

43 Dukes, 1885, 164–66.

44 "Drug Traffic in Shanghai," *North China Herald,* 14 July 1923, 133.

45 Farrère, 1904, 143.

Intoxicating Fumes

1 Gautier, 1907 (1835–36), 222.

2 Farrère, "Les Pipes," *Fumée d'opium,* 1904, 160; and Farrère, 1905, 57.

3 Magre, 1922, 77–78; Desnos, 1943, 84; and Kipling, 1899, 305.

4 Gautier, 1972 (1838), 22 and 25.

5 Cocteau, 1957 (1930), 72.

6 No. 6606, 1914, 31.

7 Farrère, 1904, 4.

8 Kane, 1882, 34.

9 Colton, 1926, Act III, 184.

10 Kane, 1882, 45; and Cooke, 1860, 125.

11 Malraux, 1934 (1933), 279. Opium and antiques dealer Baron de Clappique is speaking to the opium addict Old Gisors.

12 Rapaport, 1995, 70.

13 Kane, 1882, 43.

14 Dukes, 1885, 164.

15 Lawrence, 1870, 240.

16 Malraux, 1934 (1933), 241. Ellipses in original text. The character Ferral is speaking to the opium addict Old Gisors.

17 Kane, 1882, 41, 42; Beck, 1898, 163; and Greene, 1980, 142.

18 Rohmer, *Dope,* 1917, 117; and Rohmer, *The Yellow Claw,* 1917, 152.

19 Rohmer, *Dope,* 1917, 175–76.

20 Beck, 1898, 156.

21 Desnos, 1943, 85.

22 Cocteau, 1957 (1930), 67.

23 Latzarus, 23 April 1932, 10.

24 Farrère, 1904, 263.

25 Quella-Villéger, 1989, 126 and 133.

26 Murphy, 1922, 17.

27 Kane, 1882, 90.

28 Hahn, n.d., 220.

29 "Emily Hahn," 1989, 208–10.

30 Lane, 1908 (1836), 341–42.

31 *Assam Opium Enquiry,* 1925, 37–39.

32 Lane, 1908 (1836), 342.

The Writer's Muse

1 Farrère, cited in the Préface by Pierre Louÿs, 1904, vii.

2 du Tott cited by Wilson, 1803 (1785), 29.

3 Nerval, 1972 (1851), 87 and 88.

4 Gautier, 1857, 157 and 236.

5 Chateaubriand, 1963 (1811), 151–52.

6 Liedekerke, 1984, 50–51.

7 Verne, 1989, 184.

8 Lorrain, 1994 (1901), 32.

9 Steegmuller, 1996 (1963), 156; and Rouveyre, 1945, 143.

10 Baudelaire, c. 1868 (1857), 349.

11 Ibid., 158.

12 Sydenham, 1858 (1682), 281; Pichois, 1989, 129; and Baudelaire, 1928 (1869), 14.

13 Pichois, 1989, 341.

14 Baudelaire, c. 1868 (1857), 123.

15 Cocteau, 1957 (1930), 64; and Picabia, 1974 (1924), 61.

16 Toulet, 1939, 117.

17 Walzer, 1987, 52; and Salmon, 1955, Vol. II, 224.

18 Salmon, 1955, Vol. II, 225; Vol. I, 334; and Vol. II, 224.

19 Jarry, n.d, 202–5.

20 Steegmuller, 1970, 395.

21 Cocteau, 1957 (1930), 146.

22 Steegmuller, 1970, 420.

23 Mercié, in Picabia, 1974, 18.

24 Gilbert-Lecomte, 1971, 60, 99, 137, 156, 173 and 227.

25 Colette, 1968 (1932), 15.

26 Liedekerke, 1984, 158.

27 Yvorel, 1992, 108.

28 Quella-Villéger, 1989, 128.

29 Liedekerke, 1984, 50; cited in Bachmann and Coppel, 1989, 211; Farrère, "Ce qui se passa dans la maison du Boulevard Thiers," *Fumée d'opium,* 1904, 221; Salmon, 1955, Vol. I, 334; G. Miraben, *La lutte antitoxique, la fumée divine* (Paris 1912, 81), cited in Yvorel, 1992, 187; and Liedekerke, 1984, 161.

30 Liedekerke, 1984, 159.

31 Ibid. Bachmann and Coppel, 1989, 217–18, report "L'Affaire Ulmo" as "L'Affaire Ullmo."

32 Dryden, 1962 (1681), lines 482–83.

33 Hayter, 1968, 23.

34 Ellman, 1988, 346; and Wilde, 1926 (1891), 189.

35 Liedekerke, 1984, 236, 220 and 261; and 134 and 139.

36 Symons, 1924 (1889), 3.

37 "Aleister Crowley," 1982, 202.

38 Sherry, 1994, 368–69.

39 Poe, 1945 (1838), 235.

40 Poe, cited in Stoddard, 1884, 165–67.

41 Anonymous note inserted into Barnitz, 1901.

42 Algren, 1949, 58. The speaker is the junkie Frankie, "the man with the golden arm."

Chinatowns

1 Kane, 1882, 2.

2 Farwell, 1885, 6 and 24.

3 Dillon, 1962, 30 and 62.

4 Twain, 1904, 133.

5 Carpenter, 1920, 176–87.

6 Farwell, 1885, 22.

7 Ibid., 25.

8 Dillon, 1962, 272–73.

9 Gregson, 1970, 122.

10 Gregson, 1970, 124; and Lai, 1988, 219.

11 Beck, 1898, 145.

12 Ibid.

13 King, Sessional Paper No. 74f., 1908, 15; Sessional Paper No. 36b, 1908, 1; and Con *et al.,* 1982, 87.

14 Con *et al.,* 1982, 69; and Dubro, 1992, 52.

15 Yip, 1936, 33; and Dubro, 1992, 72.

16 Glynn-Ward, 1974 (1921), 33.

17 Murphy, 1922, 30.

18 Murphy, 1922, 147; and Dubro, 1992, 66.

19 Doesticks, 1858, 151.

20 Kane, 1882, 5–7.

21 Beck, 1898, 141 and 168.

22 Kane, 1882, 5; Beck, 1898, 11; Doesticks, 1858, 151–52; Williams, 1883, n.p; and Beck, 1898, 172.

23 Beck, 1898, 172.

24 Ibid., 175.

25 Parssinen, 1983, 49–51.

26 *The Illustrated London News.* The following are a few of many references to opium deaths: 27 September 1860, 265; 24 November, 1860, 485; 1 December 1860, 505.

27 Berridge and Edwards, 1981, 195–96, 200–201.

28 *The Illustrated London News,* 2 September 1860, 265.

29 Dickens, 1870, 1 and 275.

30 Johnson, 1952, 1021, 1090 and 1109.

31 Dickens, 1870, 273. The speaker is Princess Puffer.

32 Doyle, 1930 (1887), 231.

33 Burke, 1918, 65–66.

34 Burke, 1926 (1917), 10.

Opium Hits the Street

1 Dr. Van Dyke, quoted in the *New York Times,* 1923.

2 Buell, 1925, 48.

3 Bachmann and Coppel, 1989, 220.

4 Dubro, 1992, 52; Parssinen, 1983, 210; Terry and Pellens, 1928, 745; and Dubro, 1992, 52.

5 *Sixth Biennial Report of the Oregon State Insane Asylum for 1895,* i and 6.

6 Dubro, 1992, 53.

7 Bell and Woodhead, *The China Year Book: 1912* (1912), 446.

8 La Motte, 1920, 9 and 14–15.

9 Lodwick, 1996, 135–36.

10 Courtwright, 1982, 58; and Murphy, 1922, 95 and 148.

11 Montarron, 1933, 58.

Notes

1 Michaelis, 1998, 215.

BIBLIOGRAPHY

General Bibliography

"Aleister Crowley" from *Twentieth-Century Literary Criticism*. Vol. 7. Edited by Sharon K. Hall. Detroit: Gale Research, 1982.

Anderson, Lindsay. *A Cruise in an Opium Clipper*. London: George Allen & Unwin, 1935 (1st published 1891).

Anonymous. *Points and Pickings of Information about China and the Chinese*. London: Grant and Griffith, 1844.

Assam Opium Enquiry. Cinnamara, Jorhat, Assam: R.K. Hatibarua, 1925.

Bachmann, Christian, and Anne Coppel. *Le Dragon domestique: Deux siècles de relations étranges entre l'Occident et la drogue*. Paris: Albin Michel, 1989.

Baedeker, Karl. *Baedeker's London and Its Environs*. Leipsic: Karl Baedeker, 1900.

Barbosa, Duarte. *A Description of the Coasts of East Africa and Malabar in the Beginning of the Sixteenth Century*. Translated by Henry E. J. Stanley. London: Hakluyt Society, 1866.

Baudelaire, Charles. *Artificial Paradise*. Translated by Ellen Fox. New York: Herder and Herder, 1971 (1st published as *Les Paradis artificiels*, 1860).

Beck, Louis J. *New York's Chinatown*. New York: Bohemia Publishing, 1898.

Bell, H.T. Montague, and H.G.W. Woodhead. *The China Year Book: 1912*. Nendeln, Liechtenstein: Kraus Reprint, 1969.

Berridge, Virginia, and Griffith Edwards. *Opium and the People: Opiate Use in Nineteenth-Century England*. London: Allen Lane, 1981.

Brownlow, Kevin. *Behind the Mask of Innocence*. New York: Alfred A. Knopf, 1990.

Buell, R.L. *The International Opium Conferences*. Boston: World Peace Foundation, 1925.

Burke, Thomas. "A Chinese Night: Limehouse" in *Nights in London*. New York: Henry Holt, 1918.

Burton, Robert. *The Anatomy of Melancholy*. Edited by Floyd Dell and Paul Jordan-Smith. New York: Farrar and Rinehart, 1927 (1st published in Latin, 1621).

Chateaubriand, François-René de. *Itinéraire de Paris à Jérusalem*. Paris: Les Productions des Paris, 1963 (1st published 1811).

Cocteau, Jean. *Opium: The Diary of a Cure*. Translated by Margaret Crosland and Sinclair Road. London: Peter Owen, 1957 (1st published in French as *Opium: journal d'une désintoxication,* 1930).

Collis, Maurice: *Foreign Mud: Being an Account of the Opium Imbroglio at Canton in the 1830's and the Anglo-Chinese War*. New York: W. W. Norton, 1968 (1st published 1946).

Con, Harry, Ronald J. Con, Graham Johnson, Edgar Wickberg, William E. Willmott. *From China to Canada: A History of the Chinese Communities in Canada*. Toronto: McClelland & Stewart, 1982.

Cooke, Mordecai C. *The Seven Sisters of Sleep*. London: James Blackwood, 1860.

Courtwright, David T. *Dark Paradise: Opiate Addiction in America before 1940*. Cambridge, Mass.: Harvard University Press, 1982.

de Amicis, Edmondo. *Constantinople*. Translated by Maria Hornor Lansdale. Vol. I. Philadelphia: Henry T. Coates, 1896.

De Quincey, Thomas. *Confessions of an English Opium-Eater*. London: Oxford University Press, 1902 (1st published 1821).

Dillon, Richard H. *The Hatchet Men: The Story of the Tong Wars in San Francisco's Chinatown*. New York: Coward-McCann, 1962.

Dubro, James. *Dragons of Crime: Inside the Asian Underworld*. Markham, Ontario: Octopus, 1992.

Dukes, Edwin Joshua. *Everyday Life in China*. London: The Religious Tract Society, 1885.

du Tott, Alphonse. *Memoirs of the Turks and Tartars*. 1785, cited in Wilson, Daniel. *An Inaugural Dissertation on the Morbid Effects of Opium Upon the Human Body*. Philadelphia: Solomon W. Conrad, 1803.

Eden, Charles H. *China: Historical and Descriptive*. London: Marcus Ward, 1877.

Edkins, J. *Opium: Historical Note, or The Poppy in China*. Shanghai: American Presbyterian Mission Press, 1898.

Ellman, Richard. *Oscar Wilde.* New York: Alfred A. Knopf, 1988.

"Emily Hahn," from *Contemporary Authors.* Vol. 27. Edited by Hal May and James G. Lesniak. Detroit: Gale Research, 1989.

The Family Physician: A Manual of Domestic Medicine, Vol. III. London: Cassell, c. 1900.

Farwell, Willard B. *The Chinese at Home and Abroad: together with The Report of the Special Committee of the Board of Supervisors of San Francisco, on the Condition of the Chinese Quarter of that City.* San Francisco: A.L. Bancroft, 1885.

Forbes, F. E. *Five Years in China: From 1842 to 1847.* London: Richard Bentley, 1848.

Fortune, Robert. *Three Years' Wanderings in the Northern Provinces of China.* 2nd edition. London: John Murray, 1847.

Gautier, Théophile. *Constantinople.* Paris: Michél Lévy Frères, 1857.

———. "The Opium Pipe" in *Hashish, Wine, Opium.* Translated by Maurice Stang. London: Calder and Boyars, 1972 (1st published as "La Pipe d'opium," 1838).

Gilbert-Lecomte, Roger. *Correspondance.* Preface and Notes by Pierre Minet. Paris: Gallimard, 1971.

Goldsmith, Margaret. *The Trail of Opium: The Eleventh Plague.* London: Robert Hale, 1939.

Greene, Graham. *Ways of Escape.* Toronto: Lester & Orpen Dennys, 1980.

Gregson, Harry. *A History of Victoria: 1842–1970.* North Vancouver: J. J. Douglas, 1970.

Gunther, Robert T. *The Greek Herbal of Diascorides.* New York: Hafner, 1959 (1st published 1933).

Hahn, Emily. "The Big Smoke" in *Times and Places.* New York: Harper & Row, n.d.

Hayter, Alethea. *Opium and the Romantic Imagination.* London: Faber and Faber, 1968.

Homer. *The Odyssey.* Translated by E. V. Rieu. Harmondsworth: Penguin Books, 1946.

Huc, M. *The Chinese Empire: A Sequel.* London: Longman, Brown, Green, Longmans, and Roberts, 1859.

Johnson, Edgar. *Charles Dickens: His Tragedy and Triumph.* Vol. 2. New York: Simon and Schuster, 1952.

Kane, Harry Hubbell. *Opium-Smoking in America and China.* New York: G. P. Putnam, 1882.

Kapoor, L. D. *Opium Poppy: Botany, Chemistry, and Pharmacology.* New York: Food Products Press, 1995.

King, W. L. Mackenzie. *Losses Sustained by the Chinese Population of Vancouver, B.C.* Sessional Paper No. 74f. Ottawa: King's Printer, 1908.

———. *The Need for the Suppression of the Opium Traffic in Canada.* Sessional Paper No. 36b. Ottawa: King's Printer, 1908.

Kipling, Rudyard. *From Sea to Sea: Letters of Travel, Part II.* New York: Charles Scribner's Sons, 1910.

Knox, Thomas W. *Adventures of Two Youths in a Journey to Ceylon and India.* New York: Harper & Brothers, 1881.

Lai, Chuen-yan David. *Chinatowns: Towns within Cities in Canada.* Vancouver: UBC Press, 1988.

La Motte, Ellen N. *The Opium Monopoly.* New York: Macmillan, 1920.

Lane, Edward W. *The Manners and Customs of the Modern Egyptians.* London: J.M. Dent & Sons, 1908 (1st published 1836).

Lawrence, James B. *China and Japan: A Voyage Hither.* Hartford: Press of Case, Lockwood & Brainard, 1870.

Lewin, Louis. *Phantastica: Narcotic and Stimulating Drugs.* New York: E. P. Dutton, 1964 (1st published 1931).

Liedekerke, Arnould de. *La Belle époque de l'opium.* Paris: Aux éditions de la différence, 1984.

Lindesmith, Alfred R. *Opiate Addiction.* Evanston, Illinois: The Principia Press of Illinois, n.d.

Lodwick, Kathleen. *Crusaders Against Opium: Protestant Missionaries in China, 1874–1917.* Lexington: The University Press of Kentucky, 1996.

Lubbock, Basil. *The China Clippers.* London: Brown, Son & Ferguson, 1914.

Martin, W.A.P. *A Cycle of Cathay.* Edinburgh: Oliphant Anderson and Ferrier, 1896.

Merlin, Mark David. *On the Trail of the Ancient Opium Poppy.* Rutherford, N.J.: Fairleigh Dickinson University Press, 1984.

Michaelis, David. *N.C. Wyeth.* New York: Alfred A. Knopf, 1998.

Murphy, Emily. *The Black Candle.* Toronto: Thomas Allen, 1922.

Murray's Handbook to India, Burma & Ceylon. London: John Murray, 1909.

Nerval, Gérard de. *A Journey to the Orient.* Translated by Norman Glass. London: Peter Owen, 1972. (Abridged from the original *Voyage en orient,* 1851).

"Opium" in *Encyclopædia Britannica.* Vol. XVII. 9th edition. Philadelphia: J. M. Stoddart, 1878.

"Opium" in *The New Encyclopedia Britannica.* 15th edition, Chicago, 1985.

Parssinen, Terry M. *Secret Passions, Secret Remedies: Narcotic Drugs in British Society 1820–1930.* Manchester: Manchester University Press, 1983.

Pichois, Claude. *Baudelaire.* Translated by Graham Robb. London: Hamish Hamilton, 1989 (1st published in French, 1987).

Pliny, *The Natural History of Pliny, Book XX,* Vol. 4. Translated by John Bostock and H.T. Riley. London: Henry G. Bohn, 1856.

Pomet, Pierre. *A Compleat History of Druggs,* Vol. I. London: R. Bonwicke, William Freeman, Timothy Goodwin, Matthew Wotton, John Walthoe, S. Manship, John Nicholson, Benjamin Tooks, Rich. Parker, and Ralph Smith, 1712 (1st published in French, 1694).

Quella-Villéger, Alain. *Le cas Farrère.* Paris: Presses de la Renaissance, 1989.

Quirmbach, A.P. *From Opium Fiend to Preacher.* Toronto: Musson, 1907.

Richthofen, Baron. *Baron Richthofen's Letters, 1870–1872.* 2nd. ed. Shanghai: The North-China Herald, 1903.

Rouveyre, André. *Apollinaire.* Paris: Gallimard, 1945.

Rush, James. *Opium to Java: Revenue Farming and Chinese Enterprise in Colonial Indonesia, 1860–1910.* Ithaca: Cornell University Press, 1990.

Salmon, André. *Souvenirs sans fins.* Vol. I: 1903–1908, Vol. II: 1908–1920. Paris: Gallimard, 1955.

Sherry, Norman. *The Life of Graham Greene.* London: Jonathan Cape, 1994.

Sirr, Henry Charles. *China and the Chinese: Their Religion, Character, Customs and Manufactures; the Evils Arising from the Opium Trade.* Vols. I & II. London: Wm. S. Orr, 1849.

Sixth Biennial Report of the Oregon State Insane Asylum for 1895. Salem: Frank C. Baker, State Printer, 1894.

Steegmuller, Francis. *Apollinaire.* Harmondsworth: Penguin, 1996 (1st published 1963).

———. *Cocteau: A Biography.* Boston: Atlantic Monthly Press, 1970.

Stoddard, Richard Henry. *Edgar Allan Poe's Works.* Vols. I and II. London: Kegan, Paul, Trench, 1884.

Sydenham, Thomas. *The Works of Thomas Sydenham, M.D.* London: Printed for the Sydenham Society, 1858 (1st published in Latin, 1682).

Taylor, Fitch W. *A Voyage Round the World.* New Haven: H. Mansfield, 1842.

Terry, Charles, and Mildred Pellens. *The Opium Problem.* New York: Bureau of Social Hygiene, 1928.

Thomson, John. *The Land and the People of China.* London: Society for Promoting Christian Knowledge, 1876.

———. *Dix ans de voyages dans la Chine et l'Indo-Chine.* Paris: Hachette, 1877.

Trocki, Carl A. *Opium and Empire: Chinese Society in Colonial Singapore, 1800–1910.* Ithaca: Cornell University Press, 1990.

Twain, Mark. *Roughing It.* Vol. II. New York: Harper, 1904.

Virgil. *The Æneid.* Translated by Robert Fitzgerald. New York: Random House, 1981.

Waley, Arthur. *The Opium War Through Chinese Eyes.* London: George Allen & Unwin, 1958.

Walzer, Pierre-Olivier. *Paul-Jean Toulet: Qui êtes-vous?* Lyon: La Manufacture, 1987.

Watney, John. *Clive of India.* Westmead, Farnborough, England: Saxon House, 1974.

Whitaker, Joseph. *An Almanack: For the Year of Our Lord 1879.* London: J. Whitaker, 1879.

Williams, Allen S. *The Demon of the Orient.* New York: Allen S. Williams, 1883.

Williams, S. Wells. *The Middle Kingdom: A Survey of the Geography, Government, Literature, Social Life, Arts, and History of the Chinese Empire.* Vol. II. New York: Charles Scribner's Sons, 1899.

Yvorel, Jean-Jacques. *Les Poisons de l'esprit: drogues et drogués au XIXe siècle.* Paris: Quai Voltaire, 1992.

Fiction

Algren, Nelson. *The Man with the Golden Arm.* New York: Doubleday, 1949.

Barnitz, Park. *The Book of Jade.* New York: Doxey's, 1901.

Baudelaire, Charles. "La Chambre double" in *Petits Poèmes en prose.* Paris: Garnier Frères, 1928 (1st published 1869).

———. *Les Fleurs du Mal.* Paris: Calmann-Lévy, c. 1868 (1st published 1857).

———. *Les Paradis artificiels.* Paris: Gallimard, 1961 (1st published 1851).

Burke, Thomas. *Limehouse Nights.* New York: Thomas McBride, 1926 (1st published 1917).

Carpenter, Grant. *The Night Tide: A Story of Old Chinatown.* New York: The H.K. Fly Co., 1920.

Colette. *The Pure and the Impure.* Translated by Herma Briffault. London: Martin Secker & Warburg, 1968 (1st published as *Ces plaisirs,* 1932 and *Le pur et l'impur,* 1941).

Colton, John. *The Shanghai Gesture: A Play.* New York: Boni and Liveright, 1926.

Desnos, Robert. *Le Vin est tiré . . .* Paris: Gallimard, 1943.

Dickens, Charles. *The Mystery of Edwin Drood.* London: Chapman and Hall, 1870.

Doyle, Sir Arthur Conan. "The Man with the Twisted Lip" in *The Complete Sherlock Holmes,* Vol. I. New York: Doubleday, 1930 (1st published 1887).

Dryden, John. *The Poems and Fables of John Dryden.* Edited by James Kinsley. London: Oxford University Press, 1962.

Farrère, Claude. *Fumée d'opium.* Paris: Librairie Paul Ollendorff, 1904.

———. *Les Civilisés.* Paris: Librairie Paul Ollendorff, 1905.

———. *Les Petites alliées.* Paris: Flammarion, 1947.

Gautier, Théophile. *Mademoiselle de Maupin.* Paris: Bibliothèque-Charpentier, 1907 (1st published 1835–36).

Glynn-Ward, Hilda. *The Writing on the Wall.* Toronto: The University of Toronto Press, 1974 (1st published 1921).

Greene, Graham. *The Quiet American.* New York: The Viking Press, 1955.

Jarry, Alfred. "L'Opium" from "Les minutes de sable mémorial" in *Ubu Roi, Ubu Enchaîné.* Monte Carlo: Éditions du livre, n.d.

Kipling, Rudyard. "The Gate of the Hundred Sorrows" in *Plain Tales from the Hills.* New York: Charles Scribner's Sons, 1899.

Lorrain, Jean. *Monsieur de Phocas.* Translated by Francis Amery. Sawtry,

Cambridgeshire: Dedalus, 1994 (1st published in French, 1901).

Magre, Maurice. *Les Soirs d'opium. L'Œuvre amoureuse et sentimentale.* Paris: Bibliothèque des Curieux, 1922.

Malraux, André. *Man's Fate.* Translated by Haakon M. Chevalier. New York: The Modern Library, 1934. (1st published as *La Condition humaine,* 1933).

Ovid. *Fasti.* Translated by James George Frazer. Cambridge, Mass.: Harvard University Press, 1951.

———. "Cosmetics for Ladies" in *The Love Poems.* Translated by A.D. Melville. Oxford: Oxford University Press, 1990.

———. *Metamorphoses.* Translated by Horace Gregory. New York: Viking Press, 1958.

Picabia, Francis. *Caravansérail.* Introduction by Luc-Henri Mercié. Paris: Pierre Belfond, 1974 (from a manuscript written in 1924).

Poe, Edgar Allan. "The Fall of the House of Usher," "A Tale of Ragged Mountain," "MS Found in a Bottle" and "Ligeia" in *The Portable Poe.* Edited by Philip Van Doren Stern. New York: Viking, 1945.

Rohmer, Sax. *Dope: A Story of Chinatown and the Drug Traffic.* New York: A.L. Burt, 1917.

———. *The Yellow Claw.* New York: Robert M. McBride, 1917.

Shakespeare, William. *Othello, The Moor of Venice.* Act III, Scene III.

Symons, Arthur. "The Opium-Smoker" in *Poems by Arthur Symons.* Vol. I. New York: Dodd, Mead, 1924 (1st published 1889).

Toulet, Paul-Jean. *Les Contrerimes.* Paris: Éditions Émile-Paul Frères, 1939.

Verne, Jules. "À la morphine," in *Poésies inédites.* Annotated by Christian Robin. Paris: Le cherche midi éditeur, 1989.

———. *Around the World in Eighty Days.* Translated by George M. Towle.

London: Sampson Low, Martston, 1874 (1st published in French, 1873).

———. "The Tribulations of a Chinaman in China," *Works of Jules Verne.* Vol XI. New York: Vincent Parke, 1911.

Wilde, Oscar. *The Picture of Dorian Gray.* New York: Modern Library, 1926 (1st published 1891).

Periodicals

Anonymous. "Confessions of a Young Lady Laudanum-Drinker," *The Journal of Mental Sciences.* January 1889.

"Articles of Import and Export of Canton," *The Chinese Repository,* February 1833–34, vol. II. Canton: The Chinese Repository, 1834.

"Crisis in the opium traffic," *The Chinese Repository,* June, 1839, vol. VIII. Canton: The Chinese Repository, 1840.

"Destruction of the opium at Chunhow (Chinkow)," *The Chinese Repository,* June 1839, vol. VIII. Canton: The Chinese Repository, 1840.

Doesticks, P.B. "Among the Chinamen," *Frank Leslie's Illustrated Newspaper.* 6 February, 1858.

"Drug Traffic in Shanghai," *North China Herald,* 14 July 1923.

"Expenses of the War with China," *The Illustrated London News,* 21 July 1860.

Heu Kew. "Memorial of Heu Kew against the admission of opium," *The Chinese Repository,* January 1837, vol. V. Canton: The Chinese Repository, 1837.

Honoré, Fernand. "L'Opium en Indo-Chine," *L'Illustration.* 29 février 1896, no. 2766.

Hwang Tseôtsze, "Memorial from Hwang Tseôtsze, soliciting increased severity in the punishments of the consumers of opium and the imperial reply," *The Chinese Repository,* September 1838, vol. VII. Canton: The Chinese Repository, 1839.

The Illustrated London News. 25 August 1860.

The Illustrated London News. 2 September 1860.

Latzarus, Louis. "Le Paradis des idiots," *Voilà.* Paris, 23 avril 1932, no. 57.

Lin, Tse-haü. "Letter to the Queen of England from the imperial commissioner and the provincial authorities requiring the interdiction of opium," *The Chinese Repository,* May 1839, vol. VII. Canton: The Chinese Repository, 1840.

Montarron, Marcel. *Détective,* 20 April 1933.

No. 6606. "A Modern Opium Eater." *The American Magazine,* vol. 78, LXXVIII, June 1914.

"1,500,000 Drug Users in America, He Says," *New York Times,* 14 May, 1923.

"Opium," *The Chinese Repository,* August 1832, vol. II. Canton: The Chinese Repository, 1833.

"Opium in the Army," *The Chinese Repository,* May 1832, vol. II. Canton: The Chinese Repository, 1833.

"Opium, opium dealers and smokers," *The Chinese Repository,* November 1838, vol. VII. Canton: The Chinese Repository, 1839.

Rapaport, Benjamin. "The Chinese Opium Pipe" in *Arts of Asia.* Vol. 25, no. 2, March–April, 1995.

Tang. "Proclamation respecting opium, addressed to the people of the province of Canton, by their excellencies the governor and lieut.-governor of the said province," *The Chinese Repository,* January 1839, vol. VII. Canton: The Chinese Repository, 1839.

"The traffic in opium carried on with China," *The Chinese Repository,* 1836–37, vol. V. Canton: The Chinese Repository, 1837.

ACKNOWLEDGEMENTS

The fascination with opium runs more deeply than I could ever have imagined. Many people eagerly contributed suggestions for movies, books, even their own opium experiences. I'd like to thank them, and especially the following, for their help. John Atkins, for the suggestions; Todd Belcher, for the photography advice; Erika Berg, for the photograph of the Shanghai woman smoking, the scrapbook entries and the fast work on the opium scale; Gerry Davie, for the loan of *The Dominion Illustrated;* Françoise Giovannangeli, for Paris research and help with the Paul-Jean Toulet translation; Charles Haynes, for the photographs of the Southeast Asian opium smokers; Ed Leimbacher, of Mister E Books in Seattle; Sarah Malarkey, for her enthusiasm; Sean Rossiter, for the information on Mackenzie King; Candace Savage, for the tip about Judge Emily Murphy's *Black Candle,* the photograph of the opium smoker and for the 1933 *True Detective Mysteries*; Blair Shakell, for the loan of the vintage paperbacks.

And special thanks to Saeko Usukawa, my editor, for the steady stream of suggestions and references, and for the tight editing; to Don Stewart of MacLeod's Books in Vancouver, for alerting me to the sale of the opium pipes, for the loan of Park Barnitz's *The Book of Jade* and for his much appreciated interest and help; and to David Gay, whose persistence in the search for opium images almost exceeded my own.

This page: Border decoration from a brief mention of opium in China in *The Illustrated London News,* 20 July 1907, p. 129.
Facing page: "Opium Smoker," from E.J. Dukes, *Everyday Life in China* (1885), p. 163.
Page 152: "Manner of Smoking Opium," engraving from S. Wells Williams, *The Middle Kingdom* (1899), p. 385.

INDEX

Manner of Smoking Opium.